Visiting the Dog Park

Having Fun, Staying Safe

CHERYL S. SMITH

<figure>Dogwise™ Publishing</figure>

Wenatchee, Washington U.S.A.

Visiting the Dog Park. Having Fun, Staying Safe
Cheryl S. Smith

Dogwise Publishing
A Division of Direct Book Service, Inc.
701B Poplar St.
Wenatchee, Washington 98801
1-800-776-2665
www.dogwisepublishing.com / info@dogwisepublishing.com

© 2007 Cheryl S. Smith

Photographs by: Cheryl S. Smith, Elaine Diedrich,
Donn Dobkin-www.justamomentphoto.com, dogs.yowser.org
Illustrations by Terry Ryan, Judith L. Winthrop
Indexing by Cheryl S. Smith

Limits of Liability and Disclaimer of Warranty:
The author and publisher shall not be liable in the event of incidental or consequential damages in connection with, or arising out of, the furnishing, performance, or use of the instructions and suggestions contained in this book.

Library of Congress Cataloging-in-Publication Data
Smith, Cheryl S.
  Visiting the dog park : having fun, staying safe / Cheryl S. Smith.
    p. cm.
  Includes index.
  ISBN-13: 978-1-929242-45-0 (alk. paper)
  ISBN-10: 1-929242-45-X (alk. paper)
  1. Parks for dogs. 2. Dogs--Training. I. Title.
  SF427.45.S65 2007
  636.7'0835--dc22

                                        2007002755

ISBN: 1-929242-45-X
Printed in the U.S.A.

Contents

IN A PERFECT WORLD

In a perfect world, there would be no need for dog parks. All dogs would be so well mannered that they could play off leash on any patch of ground and be so well trained that they could respond immediately to any commands from their people. Restaurants, movie theaters, and friends would welcome your perfectly mannered companion and peace and harmony would abound. In a somewhat less than perfect but still idealized situation, dog parks would be set aside for off-leash play and all dogs and owners would use them wisely and without incident. While many dogs have a great time and benefit from their dog park experiences, in the real world, unfortunately, all doesn't always go smoothly and according to plan. This is where the controversy about dog parks arises. Dogs and people have been attacked and bitten. Dogs have even been killed by other dogs in the park. Communicable diseases have been passed from dog to dog. Humans have not kept up their part of the bargain, failing to clean up or obey the rules. Your opinion of dog parks probably depends on your own experience (or lack thereof) with them.

In most parts of the country, you have more opportunities now to try out a dog park than in the past. Dog owners across the country are gathering together and petitioning local governments for a patch of open space for their canine companions at an increasing rate. Sections of already-existing parks are being partitioned off, and new spaces are being developed at a lively pace. With yards the size of postage stamps and neighborhood covenants outlawing solid fences, many dog owners don't have a safe place to play with their pups off-leash even on their own property. More and more people are turning to public property and arguing that they deserve the same consideration for their avocation (dogs) as do those playing such sports as tennis or softball or parents wanting playgrounds for their children.

So maybe you're eager to get out in the dog park. You've heard from friends how much their dogs love it and you want to be sure it's the enjoyable experience you picture for your dog. The fact is some dogs just aren't right for dog parks, and others need a little assistance to appreciate the social opportunity. You will be better able to see that all goes well for your dog if you have some essential knowledge of dog parks before venturing through the gate.

Think back to a first day of school that you've witnessed. Some kids charged toward this new adventure with glee, others were upbeat but more reserved, some hung around the edges in trepidation, and others had a complete meltdown. Being human children rather than dogs, they were sent back to school day after day regardless of their response but (hopefully) with compassionate support and soothing reassurances. Though there may have been tears and fights along the way, most eventually adjusted to the experience. But there were probably some who never really fit in.

Dogs have a parallel experience when visiting a dog park. Some dogs participate in dog park play enthusiastically and appropriately. Some take a bit longer to warm up to the environment but eventually become active playmates. Others just never seem to fit in. You may think of dog parks as fun—and many dogs agree with you—but some dogs find them overwhelming and frightening. This book is written to help you decide if a dog park is right for your dog and to show you how to make the most of your dog park visits by preparing for the experience. While the information I have included in this book on training, dog park design, and strategies to minimize problems may help your dog enjoy the park, some dogs are never going to have a successful dog park experience. If so, find other ways to have fun with your dog. . .ways your dog appreciates more.

I am neither a proponent nor opponent of dog parks. I understand the potential hazards that lead many dog professionals to advise (sometimes strenuously) against using a dog park, but I also understand the need for off-leash canine opportunities in our increasingly crowded society. Dog parks are no better or worse than the designers who develop them and the people and dogs who visit them. While many dogs enjoy the exercise and social opportunity the dog park offers, this book will look at how to make the experience as safe and beneficial as possible. There are some criteria and training ideas for both ends of the leash, rules everyone should obey, and practical information on how to avoid diseases.

Dog parks can be a boon to canines and their humans. Help them fulfill their potential by following the guidelines given here, and encouraging others to do the same.

Friends on their way to the dog park.

Chapter 1

DOG PARKS: WHO SHOULD AND SHOULDN'T USE THEM

Mention "dog park" and most people picture a fenced area, with dogs running free and playing with each other. But this isn't the only model for dog parks. Some are off-leash play areas, but unfenced. Some are fenced, but meant to be used by one dog/handler team at a time, to get some exercise or practice some training. A few are private, with only a certain clientele allowed. A few municipal parks require people  to earn the privilege of using the park, then they are issued a key or given the combination to the lock on the gate. Most are wide open to public use.

In this book, we will be discussing the common conception of a dog park. This is a fenced area of ground, to be used by off-leash dogs (and their owners) for exercise and play. Who goes to the dog park and how they behave once there impacts how successful the park is in day-to-day use. The most basic problems associated with dog parks can be avoided completely by not bringing inappropriate dogs. Dog parks are not a joyful experience for all dogs. Some would be much happier on a solitary walk with their owners. Be honest about your own dog. (See the Personality Types later in this chapter for descriptions of appropriate and inappropriate characteristics and behavior.) Always follow all rules of the park, whether or not you agree with them. People should bring themselves and their dogs to dog parks only when they can fully enjoy the many benefits they offer.

A fairly typical dog park lies beyond the fence.

The Many Benefits of Dog Parks

Public parks include playgrounds, soccer fields, softball diamonds, tennis courts, and picnic areas as a matter of course. Yet dog owners often have to fight for space and permission to use them. Anti-dog sentiment often runs high. Perhaps this will change as more of those in authority realize that dog owners are an increasingly active group and that well designed and managed dog parks are not a public nuisance, but an asset. And the benefits extend to both dogs and humans, and even to non-dog people.

The first benefit most people think of is exercise. Trainers have a saying that "a tired dog is a good dog," and that is true to a large extent. With many dog owners living in apartments and with many houses having very small yards, dogs need public spaces to stretch their legs and burn off their energy—especially dogs who are left alone at home for long periods of time.

Nearly as important as exercise is socialization. While dogs love to spend time with their humans, most still benefit from regular interaction with their own kind. Dog parks offer the advantage of allowing dogs to be off leash, so they can react to each other more naturally, without the tension of a leash. Dogs also have the opportunity to encounter a variety of people in a dog park, making them more at ease with people of all kinds and sizes.

Dedicated enclosed play areas for dogs keep them separated from other park users. So those who would rather avoid dogs can, and dog owners don't have to sneak onto ball fields to try and get some exercise. Groups of dogs and their owners can also act as a passive crime deterrent. Active dog parks mean lots of people coming and going and more sets of eyes keeping watch.

Dogs bring people together. In many communities, people are reluctant to speak with a stranger. Having dogs to talk about provides some common ground and helps to break the ice. Dogs are so effective at this that there is a category of service dogs known as "social dogs." Used mostly with handicapped children, the dogs are there to facilitate social contact with other children. It works just as well with adults. Studies have shown that adults walking dogs in parks have more social interactions with other park users than did those walking without dogs.

Many people enjoy watching dogs play. Some dog lovers may be living in situations where they cannot currently have a dog of their own. A visit to the dog park lets them get a "dog fix" and perhaps form a mutually beneficial friendship with a dog owner.

People are more motivated to get out and get some exercise when they can take their dog with them. The dog park itself may or may not be good for exercise, depending on its size and layout. But getting out and getting there is better than sitting at home, and play in the park can also contribute.

The many park users who understand that a dog park is a privilege they have to work to keep will oversee the actions of other dog owners and apply pressure to conform to rules. The result is fewer dog-related problems are likely to occur in the vicinity of the dog park. Dog owners given space for their avocation—on a par with ball players, parents with young children, skateboarders, etc.—feel better served by their local government and may be more civic-minded citizens.

Both dogs and humans are more content when allowed to pursue their desired activities.

Who Can Take Best Advantage of Dog Parks

First, let's consider the dogs. Before a dog is brought to a dog park, he or she should have some basic training. Why? Well, presumably you want to leave after some period of time, preferably with your dog, right?! If you can't call your dog to you, you may be in the dog park for much longer

than you planned as your dog continues to enjoy playing...
and staying away from you. If any sort of trouble breaks
out, you want to be able to call your dog to you and away
from whatever is going wrong. If your own dog starts to get
a little out of control, you should be able to call her over and
have her settle down, or be able to easily take her out of the
park. Most or all of these skills can be learned if you attend
group dog training classes, the format used by most trainers.
You want your dog to gain some experience at being under
control and to pay attention to you in the presence of other
dogs.

*Dog parks provide a place for dogs to socialize and exercise off
leash.*

Dogs should already be well socialized before you turn
them loose in a dog park. If you have not observed your dog
interacting with a variety of other dogs and other people,
how do you have any idea what is going to happen when
you turn him loose in a dog park? Dogs that have dem-
onstrated that they enjoy socializing with others in more

controlled situations will be more likely to also enjoy the dog park experience.

Some dogs are just innately better suited to the dog park experience than others. You should know your own dog. See the Personality Types section later in this chapter and decide which description best fits your dog. If your dog is self-assured but not overbearing, friendly but not overly exuberant, and able to pay some attention to you in the face of distractions, you have the best chance of enjoying the experience.

To shift focus to the humans involved, there is plenty of responsibility when visiting a dog park. You need to be committed to keeping an eye on your dog, while also being observant of other dogs and owners. You should have at least a basic understanding of canine body language so that you can spot trouble early and head it off before it gets any worse. And you should always be willing to leave—or not to go into the park in the first place—if things are not going well.

Dogs Who Are Unlikely to Benefit from Dog Parks

While it may be hard to admit that your dog may fall on the "should not" side of the equation when it comes to visiting a dog park, bringing the wrong dog makes for a bad experience for everyone. Please stay away if you fit any of these categories.

Puppies who have not yet had their shots

This is only a temporary condition, of course. But to avoid exposure to diseases the puppy may not be protected against, such as parvovirus, wait until he or she is older. Some veterinarians say it's all right to visit once your puppy has had the second round of vaccinations, while others insist you wait to complete the third set of shots. This is a detail you should discuss with your veterinarian. Puppies can also react very strongly to a bad experience, and form an outlook that will last for life, so you must be very careful to make any dog park experiences good ones.

Females in heat

Another temporary condition. It may seem unfair to have to keep your dog away when she has done nothing wrong, but there's just too strong a possibility for those raging hormones to lead to problems. Fights could erupt, or you could find yourself with your female being bred by one of the intact males at the park. It's far wiser to stay away until life returns to normal.

Fearful dogs

How fearful is too fearful? It might help to think about the difference between caution and fear, between the Wallflower and the Nervous Nellie described in the Personality Types section. A cautious dog in a dog park may stay on the outskirts, avoid groups of dogs, and eventually choose some other single dog with whom to interact, or may stay unengaged but enjoy sniffing around in solitude. A truly fearful dog will also avoid the other dogs in the park, but will be focused solely on that task and will not find any enjoyment in the experience. Fearful dogs will fight if cornered, so are not safe to bring into a group situation.

Aggressive dogs

Again, this can be a gray area, but an even more important one to figure out and get right. Aggressive dogs have no place in dog parks, whether they're dog aggressive, resource guarders, or aggressive toward humans. You have to be honest to make this call. While a dog should certainly be allowed to tell a dog who is being pushy to back off, that should be no more than a quick bark or snarl and perhaps an air snap. Any dog who does more than that does not belong in a dog park.

Bully dogs

These dogs are not aggressive in the true sense of the word, but they can be just as disruptive. They play too rough, insist too much that others play with them, refuse to accept requests to be left alone, and just generally create chaos in the dog park. If you have a bully dog and want to visit a dog park, you will need to control your dog closely so that you are not a bother to everyone else there.

Humans Who Are Problematic in Dog Parks

All these human shortcomings can be changed with some effort, but take a look at yourself and see if you have any of these tendencies.

Humans who only want to socialize

There's nothing wrong with socializing, and if you come to know the regulars at a park you'll have a better idea of who'll be there when and who gets along best. But you can't devote all your attention to your social circle and forget about the dogs. You have responsibilities here.

Humans who won't obey the rules

All dog parks need rules, and nearly all the rules are there for a very good reason. But even those you may think silly should be observed. Dogs are easily targeted for exclusion from public places, and people have usually invested a lot of effort into gaining a dog park. Anyone who invites

official disapproval by breaking rules may find themselves
banned.

Humans who can't control their dogs
You should at the very least be able to call your dog to
you and take away any object he or she may have. Dog parks
can be a great place to practice your good manners training,
but you need to have done some training first. If a fight
breaks out, it could escalate quickly if dogs are allowed to
"pack up" in a sort of mob mentality, or it can be nipped in
the bud by dogs being called to their respective owners.

Fortunately, the majority of dogs and owners probably
don't fit any of the preceding categories, and will be candi-
dates for good, safe visits to a dog park.

Personality Types That Fit (or Don't Fit) Dog Parks

While reading the following descriptions, you may recognize schoolmates, co-workers, family, and friends. You
should also recognize dogs you have known. We share re-
markably similar personality traits. Obviously, some types
are better suited to the environment of the dog park than
others. So consider which category best describes your dog,
and if a visit to a dog park will be a welcome outing. Note
that the mention of specific breeds is a generalization and
may not fit particular dogs of any given breed. The breeds
are only mentioned in an effort to help you picture the personality being described.

The Social Butterfly
This individual thrives on social contact. It doesn't matter if the crowd contains long-time friends, casual acquaintances, or total strangers, it's all fine with the social butterfly.
He or she can occasionally create problems by approaching

a less self-assured individual too directly, but there's no ill will at all. This personality type is a good candidate for a dog park. Golden Retrievers or Papillons may come to mind when picturing the social butterfly.

The Machismo Mugger

Less polite than the Social Butterfly, this type also thrives on contact, but definitely comes on too strong. Sometimes this is a breed trait—Labrador Retrievers are frequent culprits—and while individuals within the breed may do okay with the rough greeting, other breeds or mixes of breeds may object. Others have called this type Tarzan (no social graces) or Tim the Toolman (ditto). This type would be good with a play group that tolerates the lack of social graces.

The Rugged Individualist

This type goes his or her own way. The behavior may appear somewhat antisocial, but actually the Individualist is mostly neutral toward others (Afghan Hounds and Lhasa Apsos are good examples), or focused on a specific task or goal. That goal may be obvious, like the ball-crazy retrievers or Frisbee-fetching Border Collies, or less intense, such as checking all the smells along a regular route. As long as they're not harassed by others, Individualists appreciate the freedom but not always the company at a dog park. Visiting the park during off-peak times might be especially important for these dogs.

The Wallflower

They'd really like to join in some of the fun, but they aren't quite sure they will be accepted by their peers. So they hang around the edges, maybe trying to find another individual who's unengaged. Some Collies and Pomeranians may fit this bill. Visiting the park at times of lower use can help them handle the experience, and arranging play dates with an established friend or two is an excellent idea. Be prepared to leave if the action gets to be too much.

A variety of personality types are evident in this photo. See if you can spot a Nervous Nellie, a Wallflower, and a couple of Social Butterflies.

The Rabble Rouser

This type craves action, and isn't too particular about how he or she gets it. A riot is better than a nap in the sun, and if the Rabble Rouser has to create the riot, that's okay with him. The Rabble Rouser might also be called a Juvenile Delinquent, but it's not always something that changes with age. This type can easily disrupt an entire dog park, ruining the experience for everyone else, and should be kept away unless the owners are sure they can control them. Some (but of course not all) Jack Russell Terriers and Welsh Corgis may fit this overly exuberant bill.

The Nervous Nellie

You might think this is the same type as the Wallflower, but this individual is not looking to join the fun. He or she doesn't even see the dog park action as fun—it's too scary. Shy Shetland Sheepdogs and anxious Chihuahuas might be some examples. This dog will not enjoy the dog park experience, and may feel she has to defend herself if cornered by other dogs. Find other things to do with this one.

Small Dogs in Dog Parks

Most toy dog experts are adamantly against bringing these little dogs into one-size-fits-all dog parks. They see the hazards as too great to be offset by any benefits. And they are certainly right that the risks increase for smaller dogs. The largest risk is injury, and it could happen for a number of reasons:

- Small dogs can be viewed as prey by larger dogs.

- Small dogs can be "run over" by large dogs playing hard.

- Small dogs can be tripped over/kicked by humans who are not looking down.

- Small dogs can be injured by rough play they are engaging in.

- Small dogs can be more susceptible to weather conditions, and may suffer heat stroke.

- Small dogs may escape through fences that keep other dogs safely contained.

A dog park section devoted specifically to small dogs lets the smaller canines play together without fear of bigger dogs running them over.

Various other problems can also occur:

- Owners of small dogs may face social pressure to "let them work it out" when their dog is bullied by a larger dog.

- Small dogs can develop insecurities/anxieties after bad experiences at the dog park.

- A scared small dog can hide in a larger dog park, not responding to the owner, and be difficult to find.

- Owners of small dogs may pick the dog up in an effort to protect him or her, and possibly find themselves under attack.

- Small dogs held in the laps of their sitting owners may feel empowered to behave in an antisocial aggressive manner toward any dogs that come near.

So must you stay away from dog parks if you have a small dog? Unless some additional criteria can be met, the answer could be yes for safety's sake.

The optimum condition is a dog park that has a separate area specifically for small dogs. These make up only a small percentage of existing parks, unfortunately. If no park near you has such an area, you may need to petition for one.

Second best to a specific area is a specific time. This, of course, won't fit everyone's schedule, and if it's a popular time when the park sees heavy use, owners with larger dogs may sneak in.

If there is no specific area or specified time, owners of small dogs can get together to form a play group. With enough people, and a time that isn't when hordes show up to use the park, you may be able to politely ask others to give your small dogs 20 minutes or so in the park without any larger competition. Post your most diplomatic owners at the gates to speak persuasively to others who may arrive.

Even less safe is just trying to visit the park on your own at times of lower use. You may not have much warning of other arrivals. A large dog could be charging in at your small dog before you know what's happening. Even if you are close enough to snatch your dog up, this can possibly create even more problems. Some dogs, even well-meaning social ones, may try to climb your body to meet your dog. You could be knocked down or injured. Your own dog might feel either panicked or empowered, and could also hurt you, either in trying to get away or trying to attack the other dog. This is a situation to be avoided for sure.

While the impulse to socialize dogs is an excellent one, the hazards for small dogs in general-use public dog parks are many. Owners of small dogs should either petition for a space or time of their own at the park or should meet instead in private yards of small dog owners.

Chapter 2
DOG PARK DESIGN AND RULES

The typical dog park is a fenced rectangle of open ground. Unfortunately, this is not the best design to help assure good use of the park. Certain design features lead to improved safety for all and some just offer more convenience. When visiting a dog park for the first time, stop outside and assess how many of these features it has. Not to say that you won't go in even if it lacks some of the most basic recommendations, if it's the only park available to you. But you should be aware of the increased risk ineffective design can bring.

Welcome!
BANDIX DOG PARK RULES

YOU ARE LIABLE FOR ANY DAMAGE OR INJURY INFLICTED OR CAUSED BY YOUR DOG(S).

PICK UP YOUR DOG WASTE AND PLACE IT IN THE GARBAGE CONTAINER PROVIDED.

YOU MUST KEEP YOUR DOG(S) LEASHED IN THE DRIVEWAY AND PARKING AREAS, AND YOU MUST CARRY A LEASH WHILE IN THE PARK.

YOU MUST SUPERVISE YOUR DOG(S) AND KEEP THEM IN VIEW AND HAVE THEM UNDER VERBAL COMMAND AT ALL TIMES.

FEMALE DOGS IN HEAT ARE NOT PERMITTED IN THE PARK.

KEEP YOUR DOG FROM DIGGING HOLES.

AGGRESSIVE DOGS ARE NOT PERMITTED IN THE PARK. DOGS MUST BE REMOVED IMMEDIATELY AT THE FIRST SIGN OF AGGRESSIVE OR BOTHERSOME BEHAVIOR.

CHILDREN UNDER 14 MUST BE ACCOMPANIED AND CLOSELY SUPERVISED BY AN ADULT.

HORSES AND WHEELED VEHICLES (BICYCLES, ETC.) ARE NOT PERMITTED IN THE PARK.

JOINTLY DEVELOPED BY
KITSAP DOG PARKS, INC.
AND
FACILITIES, PARKS AND RECREATION
360-337-5350

Features of Good Dog Park Design

Let's talk about our dream dog park, one with features that give the best possible chance for a good experience. While it's unlikely any one dog park will conform to our dream, this information will help you assess whether this park is right for you and your dog:

Escape-proof fencing

Believe it or not, not all off-leash parks are fenced. Do not turn your dog loose in the absence of fencing unless you are far from hazards such as traffic and quite sure of your ability to get your dog back.

Double entry gates

Sort of a safety airlock for the park, you can enter the first gate, close it behind you, unleash your dog, and then open the gate into the dog park. Without the safety of an airlock arrangement, dogs can too easily end up outside the fence.

A double entry gate is a feature of a well-designed dog park.

More than one entrance/exit gate

This prevents crowding that occurs if there is just one entrance/exit since dogs will often rush to meet the newcomer, resulting in a swirling mass of dogs as you try to enter. If a fight breaks out in front of one gate, you have another way to get out of harm's way. Dog parks with just one entrance/exit, particularly if it's in clear view of all the dogs already in the park, are problematic.

Entrances/exits visually screened from the rest of the park

Another design feature that helps keep dogs already in the park from rushing each newcomer.

Adequate size

Bigger is better, especially if the park is going to be heavily used. Some dog professionals have recommended no more than 5 dogs per acre, but the "carrying load" of a dog park involves more than size of the space—size and energy level of dogs, shape and contour of the park, and other factors can also impact whether more or fewer dogs can safely use the space.

Irregularly shaped enclosure

Odd shapes work better than the commonly seen rectangles. Dogs need places to get out of the main flow of traffic and ways to take a break from or avoid high-energy, body-slamming canines.

Contoured topography

Hills can visually separate areas better than flat-as-a-pancake playgrounds.

Trees and shrubs

Trees provide protection from the elements year round as well as breaking up the landscape and slowing down those hard-chargers. Shade in summer can help prevent dogs from over-heating. Smaller trees and shrubs can also block views and break the park up into areas to facilitate play groups forming.

Curving paths over varied terrain

Many dog professionals advocate that dog parks be designed to keep people walking in order to keep dogs from forming into a pack. Some even discourage the inclusion of benches and tables in order to keep owners focused on the dogs at play rather than their human friends. Pleasant walking paths will make this more likely to happen.

Two dogs about to enjoy a trail in a dog park.

Widely spaced benches and tables

Where there are benches and tables, they need to be widely dispersed and away from entrances to prevent dogs and people crowding newcomers. This also reduces congestion in any given part of the park.

People tend to congregate and socialize around the seating area. This can create congestion if it is the only seating provided in the dog park.

Clean-up stations

Waste containers and clean up tools should be scattered around the park so that clean up is easy. Having multiple stations allows for easier access and avoids the need to approach one where too many dogs are congregating. Always bring some plastic bags of your own, just in case.

Water to play in

Water that dogs can get into, such as a pond or a stream, is a great bonus. Dogs can cool themselves off, get in some swimming (excellent non-impact exercise), or use it as a natural "time-out" location.

Drinking water

Exercising dogs should have access to drinking water. Some dog parks have piped water available. Those that don't often have a group of volunteers who see that jugs of water are always available. Sharing communal bowls has its drawbacks (see Chapter 7) so if you are concerned about disease, bring your own.

A fairly typical set-up for drinking water. The hose is a plus but the communal water bowl can present health problems.

Parking close to the site

Having parking close to the dog park shows thoughtful design. Some people visit dog parks because they don't have the mobility to go for long walks with their dog. Some dogs are so excited at the prospect of a visit to the dog park that they pull their humans from the car all the way to the park, so the shorter the distance from the car to the gate the better.

A safe, non-isolated location

Safety for all concerned is increased if the dog park is not too isolated. Some municipalities choose to locate dog parks as far from public view as possible, however this increases the possibility of crimes such as car prowls.

Regular maintenance

Mowed grass, trash receptacles that are emptied regularly, and amenities such as water fountains and benches that are kept in good repair make for a better dog park experience.

What does a lack of any of these features mean to you? Some are more crucial than others. A lack of fencing obviously opens up the possibilities of mishaps that couldn't happen in a fenced area—dogs running off and disappearing, being hit by cars, running after and biting bicyclists, and other sorts of unwanted outcomes. You need to be very sure of your control of your dog before slipping the leash in an unfenced area. Even then, areas ringed by busy streets and hosting a variety of other users simply offer too much chance of something bad happening and are not worth the risk.

These are the most crucial features of dog parks. Some are things that you can provide yourself (drinking water, clean-up bags) and so they may be less critical, while other factors might make the park unsafe. With a little thought and experience, you'll know what works for your dog.

How Dog Park Design Can Impact Behavior

Dog park design can make it more or less likely that problems will develop while playing at the park. But, as we have seen, there's no perfect dog park. You can help improve your dog park experience by being aware of common shortcomings in the design of dog parks so you can help minimize the chance of canine behavior problems:

- If the park is small, don't bring your dog in if it's already overcrowded.

A single-gated park versus a double-gated park. The double gate system is more escape-proof.

- If the park is flat and open, with no topographic features to slow down running dogs (or to use as a safety barrier), don't let the excitement level build as high as you might in a more thoughtfully designed park.

- If the park is basically a fenced rectangular patch of ground, stay away from the corners to avoid being trapped by other dogs. Even better, stay away from the fence completely to avoid unpleasant interactions with dogs or people outside the park.

- If the park has meandering trails through the woods, keep your dog in sight so you know what's happening. Remember, you may be sharing those woods with skunks, raccoons, porcupines, coyotes, snakes, or other potentially dangerous wildlife.

- If the park lacks shade, be watchful for any signs of heat distress in your dog.

- If the park has vegetation, check for any weed seeds that could lodge in feet or ears or fur. Check your dog after a visit. Also check for ticks—detaching them early greatly decreases the risk of disease transmission.

- If the only seating is near the gate, plan to keep walking (a better idea anyway) or to bring your own seat and position it well away from the comings and goings at the park entrance.

- If there is only one entrance/exit gate, wait until the dogs already in the park are engaged elsewhere before you go in.

- If the entrance/exit is not double gated, providing a safety airlock, you face the choice of unleashing your dog before entering the park or entering the park with a leashed dog. Neither is optimal. You may be able, if your dog is cooperative, to unsnap the leash but drape it under the dog's neck in a "U," with you holding both ends as you enter. That gives you some control (though the dog can easily escape from the loop), but you can instantly free the dog by dropping one end of the leash.

- If the park is muddy, be aware that you will not be able to move quickly, that you will be more easily knocked down by running dogs, and that your dog will likely need cleaning up afterward.

- If the park is hot, dry, and dusty, be especially sure to have a supply of water for your dog and yourself.

The final factor to consider is the dogs themselves. Different mixes of individuals may result in different behavior in the dog park. If you don't know the dogs in the park, take the time to stand outside and watch them interacting with each other (see Chapter 4 for more on this). At least that will give you some indication of how they may greet your dog when you enter.

Another example of dog park rules. Always know the rules before entering the park.

Typical Dog Park Rules

Nearly all dog parks have a set of rules posted at entries and perhaps within the park. Though the details may vary from park to park, here is a range of rules commonly found at dog parks:

- Dogs must be free of external and internal parasites.

- Dogs must be free of contagious disease.

- Dogs must be licensed.

- No females in heat may enter the dog park.

- No dogs with known aggressive tendencies or exhibiting aggressive behaviors may enter the dog park.

- Dogs must be spayed or neutered.

- Humans must clean up after their dogs—and remind others to do the same. In the interest of keeping the park clean, take a minute and pick up any poop piles not created by your dog.

- Handlers may not leave the park while their dog is inside.

- Handlers must keep their attention on their dog(s) at all times.

- Barking must be minimized to avoid angering neighbors or users of other areas of the park.

- Children, especially toddlers, should *not* be brought into the dog park. Some parks recommend no children younger than 12. Children should never be allowed to run with or chase dogs in the park.

- Do not bring rawhide chews or treats into the dog park to avoid resource guarding.

- Do not smoke or eat in the dog park. Cigarette butts are toxic if eaten by dogs, and food may lead to resource guarding.

- Keep your dog on leash until you get to the dog park, and reattach the leash when you leave.

- Rules differ regarding collars. Some parks specify that dogs wear buckle collars with identification, license, and rabies tags, but dogs can get caught in each others' collars while playing. See the section What toWear in a Dog Park in Chapter 6 for a discussion of this topic. Definitely remove prong or spike collars before entering, as other dogs can be injured while playing with a dog wearing one.

- Limit yourself to bringing no more than two or three dogs to a dog park. More than that and you may be contributing to park overuse. And be sure you supervise those you do bring.

- Don't bring dogs that are not your own to the dog park. You may not know them well enough or have full control over them.

- If at any time your dog becomes unruly or plays too rough, get your dog and leave immediately.

- If your dog is obviously nervous and stressed, leave immediately.

- Obey all posted rules—even if you don't agree with them. They are there for a reason and should be respected.

All these guidelines aim at keeping the dog park safe for all, and keeping the park open by not incurring the wrath of non-dog owners—not to spoil your fun. If not all of them are posted at your local dog park, keep them in mind anyway—they make good sense.

Enforcing Rules

So who enforces the rules? Often the people that originally banded together to get a dog park built keep a watchful eye over it. They certainly don't want to lose the privilege they worked for by getting complaints that threaten the dog park. Some groups have a schedule for oversight, while others just frequent the park with their own dogs and step in as needed. Either way, if someone gives you a friendly reminder to change something you're doing, you'd best listen up.

A few parks actually have formal supervision. Others have locked gates, with keys given only to those who've met all requirements and perhaps paid a fee. Law enforcement or city/county officials may cruise the park on a sporadic basis to check on any problems.

However parks are managed, please obey all rules. Dog owners are one of the few groups that seem to face socially acceptable discrimination. A few uncaring, unthinking handlers can sour public sentiment toward all dogs and their owners. Be an ambassador for canine privileges and don't give non-dog owners any reason to complain.

Experienced dog park users (and you may become one of those yourself after a series of visits!) can help newcomers understand the rules and the reasons for them. In fact, members of active dog park groups will probably make it their business to do so. If you are new to dog parks, listen to these people. They are probably the ones you should thank for the existence of the dog park, and they may have negotiated the rules with the city or county. If someone points out to you that your dog's collar is not appropriate, or suggests that your dog may need to behave a little differently (likely if your dog happens to be a Rabble Rouser type), don't get defensive or dismiss what they're saying. For example, the wrong collar can increase the risk of injuries, both to your dog and to others. The wrong dog can disrupt the visit for everyone. Instead, take yourself and your dog back outside the fence, and from there, discuss the matter with the person or people inside. If it's a behavior issue, talk about what would need to change for your dog to fit in better at the dog park, and where you might find the necessary training. Remember, the basic premise of this book is that dog parks work best when the people and dogs using them are appropriate for the experience.

If you are in the park and neglect to pick up after your dog, you will likely hear from more than one person about it. And well you should. If you see someone else neglecting this duty, even a dog park newcomer can point it out. Few things will lose park privileges faster than a dirty, smelly dog park area.

Should you happen to be an experienced dog park user, make it your business to help newcomers fit in. Introduce yourself and your dog. Offer to explain any rules or answer any questions. Point out body language their dog is exhibiting, whether it shows enjoyment or hesitation. Suggest paths to walk, or good times to visit the park. If you make them feel welcome, they will be more relaxed and more willing to listen to suggestions should any be necessary.

These dogs appear to be playing happily, but if one dog's owner objected to the other dog's play, the dogs should be moved away from each other.

Chapter 3

A LITTLE TRAINING FOR A BETTER DOG PARK EXPERIENCE

All dogs need a few basic skills in their repertoire before they should be brought to a dog park. And all humans also need to "train" themselves to do or not do certain things in the dog park. In either case, all it takes is a little training.

Think about what your dog needs to be able to do. Getting your dog to **Come When Called**, also called a **Recall**, is the most important. After all, if you have no way to keep your dog with you or get your dog to come to you, you may be at the dog park for much longer than you planned if your dog chooses to stay and play with his buddies. If you think you can simply catch a dog who would rather keep playing, think again.

Having a **Hand Touch**, also called **Targeting**, on cue (a verbal command) will help you in various ways in the dog park. You can actually use it to call your dog to you, or to keep your dog engaged with you and close by. It's easy to teach, and most dogs seem eager to practice it.

What about calming down your excited dog? If you think shouting "hey, take it easy" or "stop that!" is likely to change your dog's behavior or calm your dog down, really think again. Dogs need to be taught to **Settle** on cue before you bring them to a dog park.

Finally, you want your dog to be able to meet and greet others in an acceptable way to avoid problems with the dogs they might encounter in the dog park. Teaching your dog **Appropriate Greetings** will prevent canine misunderstandings at the dog park and nip any potentially bullying behavior in the bud. While most dogs have been handling greetings just fine without our intervention for thousands of years, some dogs need some extra help with this.

Essential Dog Park Manners/Skills

The key thing you have to understand when training these dog park skills—or any others—is that consequences drive behavior. That is, if the dog does something, such as knocking over the garbage can, and the consequences are good, finding some tasty leftovers in the garbage, the behavior of knocking over the garbage can has been rewarded and is likely to continue or even increase. To use this basic law of behavior to your advantage, *you have to see to it that the behavior you want to occur has good consequences.* This means that while training a recall, for example, you cannot use the recall to get your dog to come to you for a bath (assuming he doesn't like them), to be yelled at for having an accident, to stop chasing the squirrel on the fence, or for any other reason the dog would find punishing. Failing to understand this basic dictum is one of the top reasons for failures in training. Think of it from the dog's point of view. "Should I keep chasing this squirrel or go back to Mom and get yelled at?" Not much of a choice! If you have already been guilty of this (don't feel bad, you're not alone), you can change your behavior, i.e., the way you train, and change the behavior of your dog.

All dogs should receive good manners training (sit, stay, lie down, etc.) needed to get along in the world and there are some highly recommended training books in the Resources section for more information on general training. The focus here, however, will be on the four skills that are especially valuable in dog parks. Puppy owners note: start training now so that when your pup is old enough to visit the park, he'll be ready to go!

Teaching a Recall

The recall or come when called skill is one that every dog should learn whether you intend to visit a dog park or not. Training a recall is a fairly simple thing to do—but it's not quick—so plan to spend some time on this one.

Unless you already have a rock-solid recall, let's start (or restart) from the beginning. Begin training in a distraction-free location, such as a hallway. And you need those good consequences, in this case some tasty treats.

Walk up a hallway with your dog, then suddenly reverse directions and back up. Most dogs will turn and come toward you because there's nothing else of interest in the hallway. As soon as that happens, say "Puppy, close" or whatever cue or verbal command you've chosen. We want to make this new cue as failsafe as possible. That means you don't use the cue unless you're sure it's going to happen. When the dog reaches you, give her a treat and praise and some scratches. Keep the treat close to your body, not stretched out away from you to the dog—you want her to come in close and allow herself to be handled. A recall isn't much use if the dog runs to you but stops just out of reach and dashes off again.

An empty dog park can be a good place to start practicing your recalls.

After you've practiced your hallway recalls for a few days, move to a slightly more interesting room (one with things that could distract the dog), and perform the same routine again for another few days. Then change locations again. When you've practiced in three or four different locations, start waiting until your dog is not paying attention to you, not walking with you, and say your recall cue. By now, the dog should be eager to come to collect her reward. Be sure to make every recall worth her while. Don't forget the praise and pats—you want to keep her engaged with you.

Slowly work up to more distracting environments. Choose very carefully when you make the leap from indoors to outdoors. The great outdoors is way more distracting than any room in your house. You may want to have your dog on a loose leash and go back to walking with her then reversing and backing up. Whenever you make one aspect of a behavior more difficult (a more distracting environment), you want to make other aspects easier (walking beside the dog rather than twenty feet away).

After you've practiced in the more distracting environment for a few days, you can again increase your distance from the dog. Remember that during all this training time, you have not called the dog to you for any "bad" consequences. If you need to clip the dog's nails, go and get the dog. Don't use your recall. Each successful recall should end with a treat, praise, petting, and maybe being released back to do whatever the dog was doing before you called. With so much positive reinforcement, the dog should be coming to you without hesitation.

Now you can purposefully add distractions, keeping in mind how many distractions a dog park will contain. Call your dog when she is playing with a ball. Give her a treat and a quick pat, then send her back to play some more. When this is working well, call her away from playing with another dog. Again, you give a quick reward, then you encourage her to go play some more. So she gets to keep having fun, and gets an extra treat in the process.

If at any time your dog does not respond to your recall cue, make a big show of giving treats to and fussing over another dog, if one is there. If no other dog is around, pretend to eat the treat yourself, having your own little party and ignoring your dog. If your dog comes over to see what you are doing, back up a few steps, call your dog, and reward her for coming. For your next practice session, make the environment less distracting so the dog has a better chance to succeed. Gradually work your way up to a more distracting environment again.

Always try to make your recall as rewarding as possible, so that those few times when you might have to use it with more negative consequences won't damage it. Don't get lazy and just use it when you really need to rely on it. Practice to keep it strong.

There are some strategies you can use should your recall fail in the dog park when you really need to get the dog to come to you (not just because you want to leave, but because it looks like a fight is brewing, say). However, these will only work once or twice, so you don't want to use them unless absolutely necessary.

The first is to run away from your dog. That's right, away. Running toward your dog will only encourage the dog to run away from you (most dogs love to play chase games). Running away from your dog may bring your dog running after you. If you can run into the airlock between the double gates, you can lock your dog into a tiny space with you and gain control. To make your running away even more enticing, run away while shouting some of your dog's favorite words (dinnertime, cookies, whatever your dog knows and loves).

The second strategy involves some play acting. Only do these things if they will not endanger your own safety with the other dogs in the park. But if it's okay, get down on your hands and knees and sniff at some patch of grass. Look really interested. Your dog has probably never seen you do this before, and may well come over to investigate. Or try a strategy that works to round up a horse running loose in a field, and may work with your dog—sit down on the ground and sob loudly. Again, the dog may come to investigate. Don't feel like an idiot—other dog people will understand.

Teaching Touch/Targeting

Another "handy" behavior to teach your dog is to touch your palm with his nose when you hold out your hand with your palm oriented toward the dog. If you can make this behavior rewarding enough for your dog, the result will be a dog who will focus on you and stay close to you when you want your dog to remain nearby. While your dog should still learn the recall behavior described above, you may be able to use a touch cue instead of your recall in some situations. Both dogs and humans seem to find training a hand touch less "threatening" and essential than a recall, so both may find the behavior more fun.

To start, hold your hand out, flat, with the palm facing the dog, about six inches in front of your dog's face. When the dog looks at or sniffs or bumps your palm, give the dog a treat. (If you use clicker training, you could certainly use a clicker to "mark" the behavior, followed by giving a treat. But this behavior is simple enough to accomplish simply by rewarding with food.) After several short sessions, reward only when the dog actually touches your hand. Take your hand away (put it behind your back) after each repetition so that the cue is presented fresh each time. Many people never add a verbal cue, using only the visual cue of the hand presentation. It's up to you, but if you want to use the touch as an alternative to a recall, it will help to have a verbal cue attached.

When the dog is touching your hand eight out of ten times that you present it, make the touch slightly harder to accomplish for the dog. Hold your hand slightly above or below the level of your dog's head. When this is successful, position your hand farther from your dog for the touch. Again, stay at this distance until your dog is successful eight out of ten times.

If you choose to add a verbal cue, first say your cue word ("Touch"), then present your hand target. Reward when your dog touches. It's essential that you say the word before presenting your hand. If you give the visual target and say the cue at the same time, the dog will only attend to the visual target and not even hear what you are saying. Practice this for several days, then begin practicing in different locations, and at varying distances from your dog. Always keep it fun for your dog, and you should have a reliable hand touch in no time. (If you would like further details for teaching a hand touch, and a variety of other targets and their uses, see the book *Right On Target!* by the author and Mandy Book mentioned in the Resouces.)

Teaching the touch behavior is easy. Just hold your hand out flat and reward the dog for touching your hand—it will become a great way to keep your dog close to you.

Teaching Settle

Having a dog who can settle, or relax on cue is also valuable not just at the dog park, but for life in general. You could use it to ask your dog to be calm when company arrives, when workmen are somewhere in or on your home, when play between kids and dogs is getting a little too rough, or in a variety of other circumstances. The AKC Canine Good Citizen test used to include an exercise in which the handler had to get their dog revved up, then show they could settle the dog back down. Trainers were disappointed when this part of the test was dropped. But you can still do it for yourself.

Teaching a settle can begin at home. Wait for a time when you and your dog are lounging quietly around the house, then go sit with your dog. Either stroke gently down the side of the breastbone on the chest or make little circles over the dog's large muscles on the hips or shoulders. This should be done in a slow, steady rhythm. Talk to your dog in a soft, slow, drawn-out voice. If you were going to use "relax" as your cue, it should come out as "relaaaaax." You should see your dog visibly relaxing— maybe his eyes close or his head drops to the floor or he

This little dog is on a "settle" while other dogs in the park continue to play.

falls onto his side. Or maybe you just feel the muscles under your fingers soften.

When you are finished practicing your "settle," remember to release your dog. Release means your dog is now free to move, however he may choose to just remain in place if he is enjoying himself.

Next, start your settle routine when your dog is a little more jazzed up, using your voice and touch to help bring the energy down. Remember to keep everything slow and quiet and soothing. Breathe deeply to help keep your own energy levels down. Praise with long drawn-out words like "gooooood."

As you practice more, this should start to become a conditioned response, so that when you begin to go into your relaxation routine, the dog settles more and more quickly. Don't use treats for this one, as they work against the completely relaxed attitude you want. Praise and touch will work for you.

Gradually start with your dog more and more excited, being careful to go in small increments. Eventually, you can alternate between jazzing your dog up and calming her down. By then, you should be able to call her away from play at the dog park and ask her to relax for a moment to lower the frenzy level before sending her back to play.

Appropriate Greetings and Bully-Busting

Dogs that have boisterous, bordering on aggressive, greetings may be at risk for fights in the dog park. This behavior may also be an indication that you have a budding bully. With early intervention, you may be able to nip that behavior in the bud. These methods won't work with a dog already well-practiced at behaving this way, but with a younger dog you may be able to change the behavior before it becomes engrained. If your dog is a long-time bully you should visit a professional trainer or behavior consultant. Start out by teaching your dog what trainers call a time-out cue. This is a cue that lets the dog know that what he is doing is not acceptable at this time and that you are going to take action to remove him from whatever is stimulating him to misbehave. Have your bullying dog drag a long line so that you can get hold of him easily without poisoning your recall cue. Let him play with a reliable even-tempered dog. As soon as you see your dog displaying any bullying behaviors, say your warning cue (such as "time-out"). Of course that will initially have no effect on the dog but it will come to serve to let the dog know that when he hears that cue, his behavior is unacceptable and needs to change. To make that point, follow the warning cue with a time-out cue ("too bad"), and pick up the long line, and reel the dog in gently for a time-out from play by keeping him away from the other dog or putting him in a crate or car.

Keep in mind this is not punishment. This is a training exercise to try and help the dog learn to have better manners. So there is no yelling or emotion. The dog simply has to stop playing for a time—one minute is sufficient—before he can try again. The verbal cues are there to first warn the dog that his behavior is not appreciated and should change ("time-out"), and then to tell him he has gone too far and is going to have a time-out ("too bad").

If the bullying behavior is not deeply ingrained, your dog may begin to moderate what he is doing in response to your warning cue. So you will see your dog starting to bully the other dog, say "time-out," and your dog will respond by changing his behavior. Congratulations! You are well on your way to creating a more reliably social dog. Continue to monitor behavior and intervene when necessary.

What You Need to Remember

You've now taught your dog several key skills so that he will have the best chance to have a good dog park experience. But what about you? Here's a rundown of things to remember when using the park:

- Train your dog. At a minimum, be sure that you can call your dog to you and ask him to settle down. You will feel (and be) more in control of a visit to the park.

- Take off the leash. What's the point of going to the dog park if you're going to put a leash on your dog? If you've done the recommended training, checked out the safety and design of the park, and observed the other dogs before entering, you've done what you can to give your dog a fun and safe experience. Leashes interfere with the natural body language of the dog, dogs can get tangled up in them, and dogs who become stressed by constant pulling against a leash can act in undesirable ways. Besides, most parks require that your dog be off-leash.

- Small dogs need special consideration. Try to find a dog park with a small dog section, or specific small dog playtimes. It's so easy for a little guy to get overwhelmed—not to mention bowled over—by larger dogs. Keep your small dog on the ground rather than toting him around with you in the park. Being elevated can either give a dog a false sense of control because of the elevated position and close human backup, or entice other dogs to jump up at the dog being held to get a closer sniff.

- Stay only as long as your dog is having fun. Visits to the dog park need to be fluid. If your dog isn't enjoying the experience, or other dogs are getting out of control, you need to leave, whether or not you're ready to leave.

VISITING THE DOG PARK 🐎

On the other hand, if your dog is having a spectacularly good time, you might want to stay a little longer.

- Be vigilant. Keep your focus on your dog no matter how enjoyable your human companions are. Don't allow yourself to be part of human clumps because that will result in too many dogs gathering in one place. It is the humans' responsibility to keep the dog park a safe and fun experience.

- Stay calm, talk quietly. Loud (and probably ineffective) commands as well as boisterous human chatter can raise the excitement level in the whole park and risk inciting some sort of bad behavior.

- Save treats (and toys) for later. There's just too much potential for dogs to engage in guarding or stealing behavior that can lead to aggression and fights.

- Provide your dog with many different forms of entertainment. If visiting the dog park is the only exciting event in your dog's life, he's likely to be overexcited upon arrival.

- Stay connected with your dog at the dog park. Not via a leash, but through a mental connection. Call your dog to you from time to time. Play a quick game, or just give him a scratch and send him back to play.

- Talk with friends. Just do it in small groups, and preferably while you're walking rather than sitting.

- Watch the dogs. You can not only learn lots about canine body language, you can also learn lessons about how to relax and have a good time.

- Always pick up after your dog. And insist that others do so as well. Pick up the occasional extra pile, if needed.

- Relax and enjoy the experience. If for some reason you can't relax (if you're too concerned about your dog's behavior, say), then you shouldn't be there. Try taking some dog training classes to get better behavior—then try the park again.

- Leave if you start to feel concerned about anything going on. Help to resolve the situation if you can, but your first responsibility is to keep your dog safe.

Chapter 4

CANINE OBSERVATION SKILLS = A BETTER TIME AT THE DOG PARK

Dog park visitors often become fascinated by the exchanges between dogs at the park. You'll often hear them comment and even editorialize about what is going on during dog play. Unfortunately, the casual observer is as likely to be wrong as right about what is going on! Understanding the basics of canine

Playing or fighting?

body language will help you become a more astute observer of what is going on in the dog park. This knowledge can lead to a more enjoyable and safer dog park visit for both you and your dog. If you would like to learn more, there are many wonderful books and DVDs available on the subject, listed in the Resources section.

Three Basic Canine Postures

Although this is a broad generalization, dogs have three basic postures: **defensive, offensive,** and **neutral**. By learning to recognize these you will be able to avoid most of the trouble that can occur at the dog park. Dog trainer Terry Ryan, author of *Outwitting Dogs* and *Coaching People to Train Their Dogs*, describes the defensive dog as carrying a shield to hide behind and the offensive dog as carrying a spear to attack with. The neutral dog is, well, neutral. She gets along with all, is relaxed and not looking for trouble. Put those pictures in your mind and you'll start to have an idea of what these different postures look like.

Defensive dogs

The defensive dog tries to make himself smaller, hiding behind that shield. Ears are flattened, head is lowered, tail is down, his whole body may be lowered. Because defensive dogs are usually nervous, you may see wet paw prints where they've walked, and they may be dripping saliva from an

The defensive dog, hiding behind his shield and hoping to make nice with others.

open mouth. A defensive dog who feels he's about to be attacked may snarl and show teeth, but it's a lips pulled back, all teeth showing sort of snarl. A defensive dog will try to escape if by himself, but in the presence of his human he may feel obligated to make a stand. A defensive dog is likely to bite if backed into a corner.

Offensive dogs

The offensive dog is up on his toes, ready for conflict. Ears are up and forward, at least until an actual attack is launched, then they may be folded against his head to protect them. The tail is held high and may be still or waving slowly. The body leans forward, held tall and stiff. Some hair may be raised at the base of the neck or on the tail. The offensive dog will not flee from trouble. He may graciously accept submissive behavior from another dog, but he will not hesitate to start a fight.

The offensive dog, always ready for action.

Neutral dogs

Think of the neutral dog as either wearing a party hat if she's the self-assured social type or walking with her nose in an open book if she's the aloof type who keeps to her own

The neutral dog, perhaps hoping to join in the fun eventually, or intent on going his own way.

solitary interests. This dog will also be standing tall, but in a relaxed manner. There is just none of the up-on-the-toes forward-leaning posture of the offensive dog.

Calming or Cutoff Signals

Beyond these three basic types, you can learn to watch for the early warning signs of stress. Behaviorists call these signs calming or cutoff signals. The term "calming signals" was coined by Norwegian dog trainer and author Turid Rugaas (see Resources). Dogs actually give out signals through body language when they are stressed as an alert to other dogs. Most (but not all) dogs are able to understand these signals when given by other dogs.

Whatever you call them, these postures and behaviors can be an indication that a dog is starting to feel tension (her own or that of others around her) and they act as a signal to other dogs to back off. These signals include blinking, yawning, lip licking or tongue flicking, sniffing, looking away, to name a few. Because these are all normal behaviors you have to read them in context. A dog who gets up, stretches and yawns, is probably just stretching and yawning. But a dog who, with another dog rushing and barking at her in the dog park, turns her head away, blinks, and yawns, is probably trying to calm the other dog down. If you think you are seeing clusters of these signals, do what you can to defuse the situation by distracting or separating the dogs if you can do so safely.

Another type of calming signal called "splitting" occurs when one dog tries to defuse tension between other dogs. When they see matters starting to get out of hand, they walk directly between the offending participants, splitting them apart. This often gives everyone a chance to settle down. Some dogs are natural "splitters," peacemakers who seem to use this behavior instinctively. Splitters are usually good

Sniffing   **Yawning**   **Blinking**

Licking   **Turning Away**

Early signs of stress, or "calming signals."

at what they do and don't get into trouble with their canine companions over it. They not only keep other dogs from fighting, they manage to avoid conflict themselves despite being in close proximity to dogs that are aroused.

The Choreography of Proper Greetings

Greeting rituals between and among dogs are seemingly choreographed, and you can learn to distinguish between proper greetings and those that may lead to trouble. In a polite greeting, dogs approach each other on a curve rather than a straight face-to-face line. A straighter approach does not necessarily mean trouble, but you should watch a little more closely when this happens. After the approach, both dogs will do the butt-sniff that so many humans find embarrassing, even disturbing. But think of it this way. If we could get as much information from a sniff (sex, breeding readiness, health information, age information, what they had for dinner last night, and who knows what else), we'd probably be doing it too, rather than shaking hands. After the butt-sniff—which should not last for more than a few seconds—the dogs should shift positions to be face to face. They may sniff each other some more, or one may lick the other's muzzle. After that, they might each go about their own business or initiate play.

Polite dogs will generally greet each other in the following manner:

- Dogs approach each other on a curve, not head on, or if one dog is approaching directly, he or she is looking away.

- Dogs sniff butts.

- Dogs reverse positions to sniff, lick, and nuzzle faces.

- Dogs either then go their own way or one or both begin to give play signals such as bowing, jumping side to side, darting in and out, and whining. More on play postures below.
- Greeting is over or play ensues.

Note how these dogs are greeting each other while curved, head to tail. This is an example of an appropriate greeting.

A greeting not going well. The dogs are too directly face to face, the Boston is staring in an offensive manner.

If you see anything other than this happening, observe very carefully and be prepared to call your dog away or physically remove him (gently) from potential trouble.

The Postures of Play

Play has its own language as well. The play bow is perhaps the best known bit of canine body language. Other invitations to play include vocalizations such as excited whimpering or barking, and actions such as bouncing toward and then away from another dog, poking with the nose or a front foot, hip slamming (where one dog abruptly turns to nudge the other dog with a hip or the butt), or assuming the "ready" position (a slight crouch that allows a burst into action). Dogs trying to get play started look like they want to play—their bodies are relaxed, their facial expressions are happy. You may have experienced some or all of these invitations to play yourself. You know how it is—your dog is looking soooo cute that you just have to stop what you're doing and play with him.

A play bow in the snow.

Two or more dogs chasing another dog could be trouble or it could be play. The first thing you can watch for is reversals. In friendly play, reversals are frequent in that the chase only goes for a minute or so before the dogs reverse position and the chasee becomes the chaser. The same should happen with wrestling games—the same dog shouldn't be on the top all the time. Watch for role exchanges or reversals. They're an excellent indication that play is going well.

Note the happy faces on these running dogs. They are obviously having a good time.

Many dogs also utilize time-outs. Maybe they're tired and need a break, or maybe they sense that matters are starting to get a little out of hand and need to be calmed down. Whatever the reason, activity suddenly comes to a screeching halt. It can be difficult to see the initiating signal, but all dogs should respect the time-out. So if one dog suddenly stops, the others should halt as well. People can help the dogs with this one, stopping play frequently to let things settle down a little.

Resisting the "Sniff"

Some dogs are reluctant to allow themselves to be sniffed, either scooting away in a circular motion to remain face to face, or sitting down. What does this mean? The first obvious answer, if the dog is an intact female, is that she is just starting to come into heat and is not yet receptive to males. But males will be plenty interested in her, and this could create problems. Remember, most dog parks have rules designed to keep females in heat out of the park for just this reason.

But if that's not the cause, what is it? Some very self-assured dogs may resist being sniffed as a sort of "control" action. They want to be the ones doing the sniffing. Nervous dogs may be insecure about the whole greeting ritual and try to avoid it altogether. If your dog is resistant to sniffing, given that it is a natural part of proper greeting behavior, your dog probably isn't ready to visit a dog park.

"It's Okay, He's Friendly"

Of the many typical things you hear at a dog park, "It's okay, he's friendly" or "He only wants to say hi" probably top the list. These are most often heard as the proclaimer's dog smashes into another dog, or mounts him, or circles around him barking hysterically. So is it "okay"? No. It's no more acceptable than a child running around hitting everyone in the room with a large toy truck while the mother smiles and says "he's just trying to get your attention." Firmly, and as politely as possible, ask the dog's human to control her dog. If the posted rules cover the situation, point that out. If the other owner won't cooperate, then take your own dog out of harm's way.

What About Mounting?

On the subject of mounting or mating behavior, mentioned briefly above, opinions about what it means and how to handle it differ. Some will tell you that it's a perfectly natural behavior, while others are horrified by it and say it should never happen. Well, hitting someone when you're angry is a natural behavior, but it's generally frowned upon in our society. So saying "it's natural" is not a valid argument. Those who are horrified by mounting most often see it as a sexual act and are embarrassed by its occurrence in public. This isn't correct either. Research (yes, people do research such things) indicates that mounting is a social behavior that occurs most often when dogs are excited, stressed, or anxious. Both females and neutered dogs do it, so that argues against a sexual component. However, does that make it acceptable? Not really. In fact, it is an obvious visual cue that excitement levels are rising too high. The dog initiating the mounting should be called away for a calm-down period.

The Truth About Growling and Snapping

Another potential point of confusion and conflict is the growling and snapping that occurs sometimes when one dog approaches another too boisterously. If it is the dog being approached that does the growling/snapping, that dog is often immediately labeled "aggressive" by other humans in the park. They've got it all wrong. The dog being approached is issuing a polite warning to the boisterous dog to tone down the rude behavior. If the dog being approached is chastised or punished for this response, a couple of things are happening, neither of them good. The boisterous dog is being encouraged in his or her rudeness. And the growling/snapping dog is learning that his or her human not only won't offer protection, but will squelch the dog's efforts to correct the other dog. This can lead to a more violent response the next time a rude dog approaches. And it will be the human's fault for misinterpreting the situation.

How Is Your Dog Feeling Today?

You must also be alert for any signs your dog is not feeling well. As you know from your own experiences when you're sick or injured, you tend to be less tolerant of those around you. Dogs are the same. Don't take a sick or injured dog to the dog park. Watch for signs of sluggishness, your dog holding herself or moving differently than normal, any tendency to resent being touched. If you observe any of these signs, stay away from the dog park until your dog is feeling better.

Test Your Observational Skills: Dog Park Scenarios

Read each of the following scenarios and decide for yourself if the behavior described is acceptable, marginal, or a definite problem. Then read on for the interpretation.

Scenario 1

The dog park is busy, with quite a few dogs and their people who haven't met each other before. A large black dog, perhaps a Lab mix, has his mouth open and tongue lolling out, tail level with his back and wagging briskly. He dashes full-speed toward a somewhat smaller black and white dog, that looks like a Border Collie. When the Lab gets close, the Border Collie lowers her ears, snaps at the air a couple of times, and then stands focused on the Lab.

Interpretation

What did you think these dogs' behaviors are saying about their state of mind? Did you mark the Border Collie down as aggressive and a dog that shouldn't be coming to the dog park? A normal human response, but one that doesn't work for the dogs. The Lab is actually the offender, coming on too strong in his approach. He's a typical Machismo Mugger. The Border Collie is well within her rights to warn him to tone it down and be more polite in his greetings. Air snapping is a polite warning, especially among the herding breeds. If no one intervened at this point, odds are good that the Lab would respect the warning and slow down his approach, the dogs would sniff each other and then either go their separate ways or initiate play. When humans misread the situation as the Lab "just wanting to play" and the Border Collie as "aggressing," they can create problems for both dogs. If the Border Collie is reprimanded, either verbally or physically, she may learn to inhibit her air snapping performance. Her human may think that the dog has "learned her lesson" and will be more sociable from now on. What the dog has actually learned is that air snapping will be punished. She hasn't changed her feelings about overrambunctious dogs, however, so the next time one comes barreling at her, she may skip the air snap and go directly to an actual bite. Herding breeds are not reluctant to bite to keep other animals—including other dogs—in line; that's what they have been bred to do. Regrettably humans have now created a dog far more likely to be labeled aggressive because giving a warning snap has been punished out of her. The Lab, meanwhile, has been encouraged to continue his boorish behavior, which is likely to get him into trouble at some point.

Scenario 2

An older woman sits on one of the benches. Her small white dog, a Maltese perhaps, is on her lap. Whenever another dog passes by, the little dog growls and snarls, showing her teeth all the way back to the molars. Each time this happens, the woman tells the dog to "Shush!" then goes on talking to other people at the park.

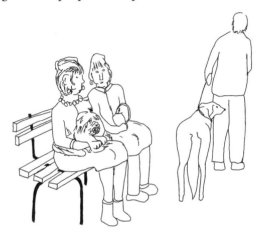

Interpretation

What did you think about this one? Is the little dog valiantly protecting her mistress? Is she feeling in a position of power by being elevated onto the woman's lap? Or is something else going on?

While small dogs often do feel more empowered when picked up by their humans, making it a bad idea when around other dogs, that's not the case here. Think for a moment about being a 5-pound puff of a dog in a place with lots of 50+ pound dogs running around. Kind of scary, right? Well, that's exactly what this little dog is trying to tell her human. Not all teeth-baring snarls are the same, and you can discover the dog's emotional state by checking the details. Dogs who pull their lips back all the way, showing their molars, are generally fearful of what's going on around them. Fearful dogs would like to get out of the situation, but if forced to remain, may bite in what they consider self-defense. The owner's reaction, telling the dog to shush and then ignoring her discomfort, is making the dog feel that she's on her own to resolve the situation, and can't count on her human to keep her safe.

Scenario 3

A father and his 10-year-old son are frequent visitors to the park with their Golden Retriever. On this day, the father is talking excitedly on his cell phone, the Golden is running with a couple of other retrievers that are regular attendees, and the son is following a large Rhodesian Ridgeback who keeps moving slowly and somewhat stiffly away just enough to stay out of reach.

Interpretation

The family's Golden Retriever is doing just fine, but the son is heading for a serious confrontation. Unsupervised children (the father's attention is on his cell phone conversation, remember) and free-running dogs can turn to disaster in the blink of an eye. The son may get along just fine with the family's Golden, but a Ridgeback is a dog of a different disposition. They can be standoffish with strangers, and this one is politely saying he would like to be left alone. If no one intervenes and the boy's behavior continues, the Rhodesian could get fed up and offer a more stern warning—which could then be misinterpreted by everyone as an act of aggression. In a worse case scenario, if the boy managed to back the dog into a corner, the dog could bite. Bringing children to a dog park is not a particularly good idea. If they do come along, for their own safety, they must be supervised even more closely than the dogs.

Scenario 4

Three Spaniels are running together, one of them carrying a ball. A Jack Russell Terrier is running alongside, barking in a high-pitched tone. A Beagle who is trotting along, nose to ground, is overrun by the four dogs. For a moment, the Beagle disappears amid the flying fur, then the Spaniels and Jack Russell run on and the Beagle stands, shakes off, and then resumes trotting and sniffing.

Interpretation

No harm, no foul here. Though perhaps the Spaniels could learn some better manners, things do tend to get boisterous when dogs play together and the Beagle just happened to get caught in the middle of their play. The occasional collision is inevitable. In most cases, the running dogs are long gone by the time the solitary dog knows what has hit him or her. One thing to be watchful for is the solitary dog who, tired of being plowed under, starts to bark and/or snap at any approaching dogs. For this dog, the dog park has ceased to be a fun place. But the Beagle in the scenario was barely bothered by the collision with the playing pack, calmly resuming his own nose-oriented activities once they had passed by.

These dogs aren't Spaniels and a Beagle, but any group of running dogs is going to have a collision from time to time.

Scenario 5

Two men are sitting on a bench, animatedly discussing sports. In front of one stands a German Shepherd. The dog's butt is pressed against the man's legs and the dog is standing very tall, ears forward, mouth closed. Whenever any of the other dogs get close, the Shepherd's muzzle wrinkles, showing the front teeth and canines, the ears flatten slightly, and she stares directly at the approaching dog without barking or growling.

Interpretation

Remember the Maltese who was showing her teeth all the way back? This Shepherd's snarl is a different matter entirely. When dogs are on the offensive, the snarl pushes the lips forward so that the muzzle wrinkles and only the front teeth and the canines show. With her position directly in front of her humans, facing the other dogs in the park, this dog is "protecting" her people, warning all others away. Shepherds tend to be very connected to their people, some overly so, and should be watched for such guarding behavior. This dog will not relax in a dog park and should share other activities with her humans instead of going to a dog park.

Scenario 6

Two women are sitting on a bench, talking about some social event. In front of them, a small scruffy dog of indeterminate breed alternates between looking up at the women, sometimes standing to put his paws on one woman's legs, and spinning to face the nearest canine. The little dog's mouth is open, tongue is pushed out and dripping saliva, and eyes are wide open. As you sit down next to the women, you notice you can see little footprint marks on the macadam area around the bench.

Interpretation

Like the Maltese in the woman's lap, this dog feels threatened in the dog park. But unlike the Maltese, he is down on the ground, left to his own devices to cope with the situation. The pushed out, dripping tongue and wet footprints are both signs of extreme stress. This dog not only is not enjoying the dog park experience, he is very close to "going limbic," meaning his brain will be in fight or flight mode, set to respond to what he perceives as a life-or-death situation. This little mix could attack a dog that comes too close, or even bite one of the women in his panic. This dog would be much happier and safer sitting somewhere without so many dogs.

Scenario 7

A medium-sized brown dog of unknown breed approaches another dog of similar size, making whimpering sounds. As they get closer, the brown dog starts jumping from side to side. He gets closer still, and rushes in to poke the other dog with his nose, and then jumps away. He repeats this act several times, and when the other dog finally responds by rushing toward him, he runs in a tight circle around the dog.

Interpretation

The brown mixed breed is trying hard to initiate play with the other dog. Everyone probably recognizes a play bow, but plenty of other body postures signal a desire to play. Hopping from side to side, jumping toward another dog and then away, poking with the nose, running off a short distance and looking back are all common play invitations. Though you need more details to be sure, the other dog rushing forward is probably an acceptance of the invitation.

Here is the poking, jumping brown dog, who now has the other dogs ready to play.

Scenario 8

A Boxer enters the dog park, which is already filled with other dogs. A group of dogs is scuffling around near the gate, and when the Boxer comes in, they rush over to the new dog. As the dogs surround her, the Boxer jumps around, trying to face all of them at once. Her human stays out of the mass of dogs, calling out to the Boxer to "play nice." The Boxer thumps one of the dogs with her front paw as she spins around, and the dog starts barking.

Interpretation

This is a hard one to interpret, but it could turn out to be a rather risky situation. A group of dogs mobbing a newcomer can cause even a fairly self-assured dog some concern. The owner would have been better advised to use another entrance if one was available, or to wait for the dogs to move away from the entrance. Now that they've entered the situation, the owner needs to be more proactive. She could call her Boxer to her and move away, or ask other owners to call their dogs. The Boxer's actions can be misread by other dogs. Boxers are fond of using their front feet, but putting a foot on or over another dog can be interpreted as a pushy move by the other dog, and might be resented. So a Boxer, acting like a Boxer, may create heightened tension levels in other dogs.

Scenario 9

A Shepherd-Collie mix and a German Shepherd are running together when another German Shepherd enters the park. The new dog joins the other two, and as they are running, they start veering to slam into each other, with a dog sometimes being knocked down and rolled over. As this continues, they start to snarl and snap at each other, and then the running stops and they start jumping at each other, mouths open, with the snarling continuing.

Interpretation

While this kind of activity might upset some other dogs in the park, it's perfectly normal and acceptable to the Shepherds. This breed's play is often full of noise and drama. They can look to the uninformed observer as if they're killing each other. But watch more closely and you'll see that no one ever actually bites anyone else, the mouths stay open, and while saliva may fly, there's certainly no blood. The Shepherds should be broken up and calmed down every few minutes to make sure matters don't get out of hand, and to keep from getting other dogs at the park too riled up.

Scenario 10

A Papillon is playing fetch with his owner, repeatedly running full speed after a small ball. A Saluki enters the park, surveys the scene, and takes off running toward the Papillon.

Interpretation

Both owners should recognize this as a situation fraught with peril. The Saluki is a Sighthound, as are Greyhounds, Whippets, Afghans, and others. They are naturally keyed to respond to movement, and readily give pursuit. They may view any moving object as prey and because the much smaller Papillon can neither outrun the Saluki nor defend himself against her, he could be in serious danger. Owners of small dogs and of Sighthounds or mixes of Sighthounds have to be more aware and cautious than others at the dog park. Training a recall good enough to stop a Sighthound in pursuit of a moving object takes real dedication and may not be realistic for most owners. The safer option is to separate Sighthounds from small dogs that could be viewed as prey. Some dog parks have separate areas for small dogs, but most don't. Check out the park occupants thoroughly before going in, and watch for new dogs arriving to be sure the park remains safe for your dog.

Scenario 11

A woman enters the park with her Border Terrier. Another woman standing alone admires the dog, saying how much she loves terriers, and reaches down to pet the Border Terrier. An Australian Terrier suddenly charges up, barking, and crashes into the Border Terrier. The Australian then stands very tall between the Border and the woman who was petting the dog, mouth closed, eyes wide and shining.

Interpretation

Terriers are generally feisty dogs and can be rather possessive of their owners. Though the scenario doesn't say so, it's likely that the woman who was admiring the Border Terrier is the owner of the Australian Terrier. The dog rushed in to "guard" his human from the other terrier, and is now warning the Border Terrier to stay away. There are no details about how the Border Terrier is responding. This situation has some potential for escalating into a fight. The terrier owners should move away from each other to separate their dogs.

Scenario 12

A Husky is running through the park with a Husky-ish dog close behind. Suddenly the first dog runs into the edge of a pond in the park, and they both come to a stop. They stand, panting for a moment, then the Husky mix sprints off and the Husky tears out of the lake and gives chase.

Interpretation

The Husky and Husky mix are exhibiting very good play manners. The dog going into the pond has called a time-out in their chase game, and the other dog has instantly respected it. Sometimes the "stop" signal is more subtle, and it will look like both dogs just suddenly came to a halt. When the time-out is over, one dog might play bow or leap animatedly around, or the game might suddenly just pick up where it left off.

They aren't Huskies, but they have called a time-out from play close to the edge of the water.

If you didn't come to the same conclusion for some of the scenarios, don't worry. You can use this chapter (along with books and DVDs listed in Resources) to learn more about canine body language (and human shortcomings) and become better at understanding what the dogs are showing you. Some of this information might just help you avoid bad situations in the dog park, and some is sure to impress your dog park compadres.

Chapter 5
CONFLICT
RESOLUTION

Most of the time dog parks operate smoothly with people and dogs doing their best to get along and "play together nicely." However, as with any endeavor, it is almost impossible to  completely avoid conflicts whether dog-to-dog or human-to-human. As social as dogs are, they can get into difficulties for a variety of reasons. Remember the personality types? The Bully can certainly create havoc in a hurry. So can the Rabble Rouser, though with less ill intent. The Wallflower can be pushed into aggression if other dogs cause him to go into self-defense mode. Even more seemingly relaxed social types can also make problems. Some dogs get overexcited when they play with others, leading to some type of conflict. Even careful owners who keep on top of things and call their dog away for frequent calm-down sessions are not going to be immune from the occasional canine dispute.

A common source of dog-to-dog conflict is "resources." A resource is anything the dog values—food, toys, their human. Any type of dog can become a resource guarder or protector if the valued item is truly precious to the dog. Humans can help avoid problems by not bringing food or toys into the dog park. But dogs can find sticks or rocks to consider their own. Be especially watchful for any signs that your dog is guarding you from others—sticking close or running over if another dog approaches you, and of course growling, snapping, or raising hackles.

And don't forget that people can have conflicts with people as well. "You aren't controlling your dog." "You didn't pick up after your dog." "Your dog is picking on my dog." Learning how to avoid or defuse conflicts however they occur in the dog park will help ensure a better experience for all.

Four Warning Signs of Trouble

Here are four situations to be on the lookout for. They fall nicely into alphabetical order, making them easy to remember:

- **Acting Out.** Any dog who is continuously agitating other dogs, whether it's through overly boisterous play, bullying, staring, or whatever, needs to be taken out of the park.

- **Body Language.** Educate yourself on interpreting canine body language (see Chapter 4) and be watchful for signs of impending trouble.

- **Clumping.** More than two or three dogs running and playing together can often lead to trouble. There may be dozens of dogs in the dog park, but most will be playing with one or two others or sniffing on their own. Large packs should be broken up by being called to their humans.

- **Dog Possessions.** Under certain circumstances, almost any dog can become a resource guarder. Watch for a dog claiming something as her own.

This situation could get out of hand. The foot over the back is a "control" movement, the Dalmatian looks a bit doubtful about it and the spaniel may get caught in the middle.

If a Fight Breaks Out

What if, despite all of your best efforts, the worst happens and a fight breaks out? If your dog is not involved, call him or her to you and get out of the area as quickly as possible. Don't wade in to try and be a hero and risk signaling your dog to join in. Shouting at the dogs involved rarely helps because dogs can misunderstand those sounds as excited "barking" from the humans, which might make matters worse and make it tougher for the owners whose dogs are involved to break up the fight. If, heaven forbid, your dog is one of the combatants, be aware that if you physically try to break up a fight, you stand a good chance of being bitten. You may end up with no other choice, but you should be aware of the potential beforehand.

Tactics for Breaking Up Fights

Loud, startling noises can be an effective way to stop the combatants. Try banging on or tossing a metal garbage can, or blowing a really loud whistle if you happen to carry one. A few people have been known to carry an air horn just for this purpose. If the dogs do break apart in reaction to noise, the owners need to leash them as quickly as possible. This is another good reason for always carrying a leash in the dog park.

Spraying fighting dogs with water can also be a good deterrent. Some dog parks have a water supply available through a garden hose. If there is a hose nearby, aiming a strong blast of water on the dogs may get them to separate. Again, once they separate, owners must be ready to grab their dogs.

Another emergency fight remedy is Direct Stop™. This is a canister of a concentrated citronella spray with a range of up to 10 feet. The spray should be directed at the faces of the fighting dogs, so you have to get close enough to reach the dogs. It works on multiple senses including smell, hearing, and sight but causes no harm to the dogs. Using this animal deterrent spray is easier and safer than trying to grab the legs of two or more swirling biting dogs. Consider carrying it whenever you are out with your dog in case you encounter trouble from free-roaming or aggressive dogs.

If none of the above tactics are available or work, you will need to try to physically separate the dogs involved. Get all other dogs out of the area first so that no new canines can decide to join the fray. Then each owner of the involved dogs needs to be prepared to grab their own dog. If people can grab dogs by their hind legs or tails and lift their back ends off the ground, that maneuver will increase the chances of breaking the dogs apart. It may also lessen the risk of being bit, though obviously it's still possible. Try and talk calmly to your dog as you are lifting and pulling—the fact that it's your voice may or may not penetrate through the mental intensity of fighting, but again, this could lessen your chance of being bit by your own dog. Do not shout, shriek, or scream. If you cannot control your voice amid so much emotion, then stay silent. Loud emotional speech will just jack up everyone's emotions more—both canine and human. If you do succeed in breaking the dogs apart, face them away from each other if possible and get your leash attached as fast as humanly possible. When all dogs are leashed, move them away from each other and unless there are obvious severe injuries, sit quietly and let everyone's adrenaline ratchet down

Post-Fight Procedures

Once a fight is broken up and dogs have been assessed for injuries, all the owners who have been visiting the dog park should take their dogs home. Even the non-combatants are highly likely to be overly stimulated by all the fuss, so turning them loose again immediately after the fighters have left the scene could be inviting further trouble.

For those involved in the fight, emotions will be running particularly high. Resist the impulse to scream at other owners, even if you believe they were responsible for the fight. It won't do any good, and will just keep the adrenaline flowing longer. Allow some time for everyone to calm down, then exchange information just as you would after an automobile accident, with the added detail of the dogs' vaccination records. The incident should also be reported to the appropriate authority, whether that's the dog park group, animal control, or the police department. Owners are legally liable for any injuries inflicted by their dog.

Human Rule Breakers

Of course, fights are not the only problem. People not following the rules are more common. Most people are uncomfortable about confronting others about their behavior, but the only way to keep the dog park a safe enjoyable place is to see that the safety rules are obeyed. Intervention is essential if you see someone behaving badly, but it doesn't have to be confrontational.

Pick Up That Poop!

Perhaps one of the most common problems is people not picking up after their dogs. If you see this happen, smile, whip out one of your own plastic bags or grab one from the dispenser at the park, hold it out to the offending owner, and say something like "I know it can be hard to find that pile if you have to walk away to get a bag. Here, use one of mine." You may receive a withering look from the offender, but most people will comply. If the person still walks away, leaving the pile in place, take a deep breath and pick up

Most parks make it easy for owners to pick up, providing bags and a place to deposit them.

VISITING THE DOG PARK

the pile yourself (it's for the continued privilege of having the dog park, after all). Make a mental note of the person and their dog and report them to the dog park group or the parks department. If you see them get in their car and leave, take down their license number.

Other Transgressions

For parks with areas specifically for small dogs, owners who bring in dogs over the size limit may need a gentle reminder. "Maybe you didn't realize that this section is based on size, not age. Your Golden Retriever puppy is really cute, but he's already twice the size of our toy dogs. There's a twenty-pound limit for the small dog run. Maybe you can find another puppy his size in the main area."

You can use a similar strategy for people bringing food, toys, or young children into the dog park. Simply point out the rule and the reasoning behind it and politely suggest they comply.

People who drop their dog at the park and leave their dogs unsupervised simply can't be tolerated. Take down their license plate number, or if they arrive on foot, note the time they usually appear, and report them to the proper authorities. You can't make any effort to reason with them if they aren't there.

Of course the toughest to deal with are the humans who bring bullies or aggressive dogs to the park. But this simply can't be ignored. Unfortunately, the owners may be as belligerent as their dogs, and dealing with them can be far from pleasant. Probably the best strategy is to form a group to approach the offender. (Note, you may have to first take your dogs out of the park to be safe.) Be polite, but firm, not apologetic. For everyone's safety, this situation can't be tolerated. If the person refuses to remove their dog, then say you're sorry, but you will have to call in the authorities because they are making the park unsafe for everyone.

Issues with Play Groups

In some communities the dog park may be the only safely fenced area of open space. Friends or acquaintances who want to let their dogs play off-leash together may come to the dog park for regular or semi-regular play groups. These play groups usually consist of dogs who have some common connection such as the same or similar breed, littermates, dog training classmates, or dogs who are familiar through relationships established by owners. Sometime these groups consist of puppies or small/toy dogs. Play groups or play dates can also develop in the dog park itself. If your dog hits it off particularly well with some other dog, you may want to coordinate and visit the park at the same time so the dogs can continue to enjoy each others' company on a regular basis. While there would seem to be no apparent problems with play groups, they can become a source of conflict at the dog park.

The dogs in this play group know each other well and get along just fine. But larger groups may not work as well.

First of all, it is a public park so you can't expect others to stay out of "your" space. Play groups consisting of dogs who know one another and are able to play rough and still mind their manners could overexcite other dogs in the park. You'll need to step in often and keep their play under control. You also have to be sure that your play group does not turn into a pack and decide to bully other dogs in the park. Like humans, dogs in a group can feel an enhanced sense of power and behave in ways they might not if they were on their own.

A few parks, though definitely not the majority, operate on a timed system, where the user in the park has the rights to the space for fifteen or twenty minutes before they have to leave and let someone else in. A play group could all enter together and share the space without having to worry about anyone else intruding. Just make sure that your play group is organized in such a way that it does not cause conflicts with others using the dog park at the same time.

Chapter 6
LET'S GO TO THE DOG PARK

This chapter will take you, step-by-step, consideration-by-consideration, through a visit to a dog park. While it recaps some information from other chapters, it morphs it into a different form, such as checklists, and some new information is sifted in as well. You should already have assessed your dog's personality type, done some basic training, and determined that he or she is a good candidate for a successful dog park visit.

The visit starts before you leave home, and ends after you leave the park. You may want to scan this chapter before your dog park visits, to help you remember how to keep the outing safe and rewarding for you and your dog.

Your Dog Park Checklist

- Choose a comfortable easy-to-clean dog park outfit, and leave most of your jewelry at home. Things that dangle can get caught on something and if it were to fall off, forget about finding it in the park. Stuff some plastic bags in a pocket so you'll always be ready to pick up after your dog.

- Decide whether bringing a toy will help or hurt your visit. Yes if you expect the park to be uncrowded and there are no rules against them. No if your dog guards his toys or you insist that the toy comes back intact. Another dog may grab and go so don't bring a treasured toy.

- If this is your first visit, choose a time of lower use if at all possible. Most parks are heavily used before and after work hours and midday on weekends. Some even post their "heavy-use" times. Coming in the off-hours will increase the chances for a pleasant, problem-free visit.

- Stop outside the dog park area and check out the design features (see Chapter 2). If there are problematic areas—only one entrance/exit gate—or basic design flaws—one big open rectangular patch of ground for a park—give some thought to how you will work around these shortcomings.

- Observe the dogs that are already in the park. If they're individuals your dog has already met and shared space with, you're good to go. If there are any dogs unknown to you, stand and watch their actions for a few minutes.

Stop outside the dog park and take a look at what's going on inside before you enter.

- Remind yourself that while socializing with the other dog owners is fine, you must always keep at least one eye on your dog, and be ready to act if you see any signs of impending trouble.

- Remind yourself to watch for signs that interactions are starting to deteriorate. By now you should be able to sort out happy, carefree play from situations starting to become tense.

- Turn off your cell phone. Your attention should be on your dog, not a phone conversation. Relax and enjoy your visit. The phone can wait.

What to Wear in the Dog Park

While there are some dog park "fashionistas," most humans come to dog parks dressed in jeans or sweats, comfy running shoes, and rainwear or other outer gear as appropriate. T-shirts proclaiming breed allegiance or dog sport involvement are frequently seen. Don't wear anything you don't want to get dirty or torn and you'll be fine. Closed footwear, rather than sandals, protects against accidental injuries from swirling dogs running over your feet.

How the dogs should dress is more the point here. Dogs with drop coats, where the hair covers their eyes, might wear hair clips to keep the hair back, making their eyes more visible to others and improving their vision. Dogs without an

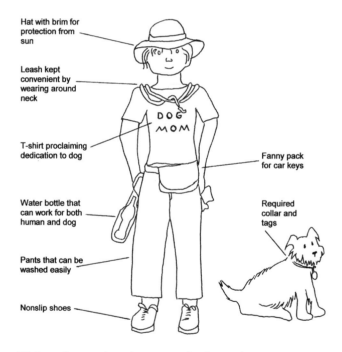

Hat with brim for protection from sun

Leash kept convenient by wearing around neck

T-shirt proclaiming dedication to dog

Water bottle that can work for both human and dog

Pants that can be washed easily

Nonslip shoes

Fanny pack for car keys

Required collar and tags

DOG MOM

All dressed up and ready to go to the dog park.

insulating undercoat, or with a lean or small body mass, may need their own outerwear to stay warm in colder weather. Material that cannot snag a tooth or a nail—so perhaps denim rather than a sweater—is preferable.

Full Monty or Collars On?

For your dog, the main "clothing" item for discussion is the collar. Should dogs in dog parks wear collars, or are they a hazard?

The subject of collars can be contentious. People don't always agree on whether they should be on or off. The majority of parks have rules about them, and you are obligated to follow them. Most dog park rules require "collars on," so you will be required to have a collar and tags. But rule-makers are often not experienced dog people. While they are thinking safety from the aspect of being able to catch and hold dogs more easily, or identify them if they should somehow get loose, they are not acknowledging the potential hazards collars bring to playing dogs.

Regardless of park rules, prong, choke, and electronic collars, head halters, and harnesses have no place in the dog park. They all create the hazard of entangling another dog in the collar or harness. A dog's teeth can get caught in the links, the prongs and spikes can injure mouths, and the dog wearing the collar can be choked by another dog caught in the collar. The electronic collar, if activated, has the additional risk of either sending a message to the dog that being around other unleashed dogs is a bad thing (because the shock doesn't always impart the message the human intends) or causing a displacement bite (where the shocked dog lashes out at the thing nearest to him at the time).

What do you do if you disagree with the rules about collars? Probably your best strategy is to agree that perhaps some rules aren't logical, but they are broken at the risk of losing the privilege of having a dog park. Be prepared for the consequences if you go without a collar. If you decide that wearing a collar is the way to go, you can minimize risk by choosing a flat wide martingale collar (less likely to snag a tooth, or to choke the collar-wearing dog if something does happen) and no dangling tags (either leave them off or, if they're required as well, use one of the little pouches that fasten them tightly to the collar.

But opinions remain divided over the wisdom of wearing any kind of collars, even among dog specialists. You will have to decide for yourself after considering these pros and cons.

Collars may be mandatory in many dog parks, but the harnesses and choke chains on the dogs in this photo are hazardous and not recommended for dog park wear.

Pros

- Collars do offer a convenient way to get a handle on a dog. If you have to call your dog to you to head off trouble, you may only have a few seconds to attach him to you physically before he decides to rejoin the fray. Grabbing a collar is certainly faster than trying to put one on.

- Collars often carry identification. Dog parks should be double gated, and only one gate should be open at a time, but accidents do happen. If a dog should get loose, identification can help get her back home. One alternative is to rely on a microchip. Though not visible or accessible to the public in general, most veterinarians and shelters have scanners that can read the chip.

- Some dogs act differently when wearing a collar than when collar-free. Just as some dogs understand when they are off-leash, and are less apt to respond to cues, some learn that "collar-off" gives them more freedom. So leaving the collar on results in better behavior.

- Some owners feel more in control with a collar in place. Because dogs are masters at reading human emotions, this extra aura of confidence translates to better behavior.

Cons

- Collars may encourage handlers to reach for them if a tussle breaks out. This can be extremely hazardous to the health of everyone involved. Any of the dogs may bite the human, either accidentally or, in a case of redirected aggression in which an aroused animal, frustrated in trying to attack the intended target, bites the nearest available thing. Sudden restraint may actually increase the level of aggression.

- Collars present a hazard to playing dogs. This is the big one that causes many dog professionals to advise that collars should be off when dogs are running free. Accidents happen just often enough for many to have seen one first-hand or heard of one second-hand. The most common is when one dog play-attacking another gets a tooth or jaw caught under the other dog's collar. Both dogs then panic and things go from bad to worse in a hurry.

- Collar tags can get caught between slats in a dock or boardwalk, or even in the crotches of trees or shrubs. A caught dog who is struggling may injure herself or trigger an attack by another dog before the handler can arrive to free the tags. This can be avoided by using pouches that secure the tags flat against the collar, or metal tags that actually slide over the collar.

Check Out Your Dog Before You Go

First, give a little critical thought to your dog's state of mental and physical health on this particular day. If your dog seems to be a bit under the weather, you should cancel your plans until she's the picture of health again. In the close proximity of dog parks, it's too easy to spread disease dog-to-dog. You know how a cold or the flu rages through a confined workspace or classroom. . . it's no different with kennel cough or canine influenza and dog parks.

Mental health is also important. If you just hosted the entire boys' soccer team and your dog was stressed by the experience, this might not be the best time for a dog park visit. You know that you're not at your most tolerant when

This little guy looks healthy and happy and ready to join the dog park fun.

stress levels are running high. It's the same for dogs. So what would ordinarily be tolerable interaction—a somewhat pushy Rabble Rouser dog running up into your dog's face impolitely, say—may suddenly become an intolerable intrusion that leads to a growl, a snap, or worse.

Something for everyone to consider is the behavior of the dog on the way to the dog park. Dogs have excellent mapping abilities, and quickly learn which car rides lead to the vet or groomer and which end at the dog park. Dogs whose only recreation is visiting the dog park often become highly excited on the trip there. You can see them dragging their humans from the parking area to the dog park. Not pleasant for the human, and not really the best attitude with which to enter the dog park. Dogs should be happy, but not hyped up, upon arrival.

Your behavior can also amp-up your dog. Doing a jolly routine when getting ready to go to the park or chattering excitedly as you approach may be too much for some dogs. Be aware if you are the cause of problems.

To counter this tendency, you should not have the dog park serve as your dog's only physical outlet. You need to do a variety of fun and entertaining things with your dog. Take walks in the woods or at the beach or an open field. Even the act of training, provided it is positive, also makes an excellent diversion for dogs. It provides some physical activity, but just as essential, it gives the dog some mental stimulation. Don't leave training out of your everyday relationship with your dog.

Take stock of your own mental state as well. If you're all wound up over some problem at work or at home, your agitated state can be sensed by your dog and may put her on edge. And you probably won't be focusing on what's going on in front of you at the park very well. If you find watching dogs play soothing, as many people do, watch from outside the park until you're calm enough to be a proper dog park parent.

Sometimes it's better to do other things with your dog. These dogs are on a walk with their owners.

Do Take With You:
A healthy, happy dog
A leash and clean up bags
A water bowl and water
An upbeat, relaxed attitude

Do Not Take With You:
  An ill or stressed dog
  Food
  Toys that may lead to guarding
  A newspaper or book

Arriving at and Entering the Dog Park

Once you arrive at the dog park, attach your dog's leash before letting him out of the car. If your dog is excited it may be a struggle for you to keep her on a loose leash! However hard she might pull you on the way, don't hurry into the dog park. Stop outside the fence and observe.

Even if this is a dog park you've visited many times before, there could be new dog/handler teams inside. It pays to pause and assess the occupants already in the park before entering yourself. If the park happens to be one of the larger examples with wooded trails rather than expansive open areas, you may be able to get some idea of how many dogs might be inside by the number of cars parked in the lot. Stand-alone dog parks obviously have their own parking lots, so if there are 15 cars already there, figure there might be 20 to 30 dogs in the park. You may even recognize the cars of the regulars. Dog parks within city parks share parking with lots of other sorts of park users, but these parks are usually smaller and more open, and you can see what's taking place within them.

After your initial overall assessment, check out the gate area. If others are entering or exiting, wait until they are clear. If humans and dogs already in the park are massed at the gate, politely ask if they could move away so others can

This owner is standing with her small dog, surveying the action before entering the dog park.

enter safely. They should comply willingly, and if they don't, they may not be people with whom you want to be sharing a dog park.

Pay attention to other behaviors of the humans within the park. Is anyone sitting and eating a sandwich? It might be all right, but be aware of the potential problems it could cause. Is anyone issuing a steady stream of "play nice, Spot; remember your manners; calm down; no, don't mount that dog, that's not nice; stop chasing that poodle" and so on? Their dog could be well mannered, in which case there's likely no problem, but you should know going in that they have minimal, if any, control over their dog. On the other hand, is anyone shouting harsh threats or commands at their dog? This attitude can sour the atmosphere in a dog park, putting both dogs and humans on edge.

Give the park itself a visual once-over to see what condition it is in. Some parks are in less-inviting low-lying areas and become swamps after a rain. If parks aren't maintained regularly, weeds may go to seed and you may encounter a meadow of foxtails or other non-dog-friendly vegetation. Be sure there are no signs indicating that herbicides or pesticides have been sprayed in the area recently.

If everything looks acceptable, then enter the first gate and close it behind you. Remove your dog's leash, open the inner gate, and follow your dog in, being sure to close the gate behind you. Move away from the gate area.

Always be sure that the gates are closed securely behind you.

Remember To

- Observe from outside the park before entering.
- Wait for the gate area to be clear before entering.
- Always be sure the gate is latched firmly behind you.
- Keep your dog on leash until inside the dog park.
- Unleash your dog as soon as you are in the dog park.
- Keep your leash handy once in the park.

Inside the Park

Remember it's best to keep moving. If you use the park as a social opportunity to meet your own friends, then walk and talk rather than stand still and talk. That helps to keep the dogs moving and avoids some of the potential problems of dog parks. If the dog park is an open area, do not meander along the fence line. That makes it too easy for dogs to get pinned against the fence or backed into a corner. Instead, wander across the middle of the space, taking care not to run into (or be run into by) other playing dogs.

You may not have thought about it, but even a medium-sized dog can knock down a human. Many dogs you will see in a dog park are just the right height to hit you in the back of the knees, and if that happens, you will be on the ground before you know it. So this is just one more reason to keep a watchful eye on all the activity going on around you. You don't want to be an accident statistic, and being knocked to the ground could even incite a fight if your own dog then feels it necessary to guard you.

If you simply must sit because your own mobility is compromised, be sure you are away from the gate and with only one or two friends rather than all the owners in the

Note the bent knees of the human as the dogs swirl around.

park. Sit as far from the fence as possible even though often seating is only available near the fences. Consider bringing your own chair and, if at all possible, vary where you sit on different visits, to avoid your dog gaining any sense of "owning" a particular patch of ground. Sitting does not release you from the need to be always aware of what's going on around you.

Stay engaged with your dog while at the dog park. You shouldn't bring food or maybe even toys into the dog park, but you can still interact with him. For example, dogs who are taught a hand touch (see Hand Touch behavior in Chapter 3) seem to find the behavior itself rewarding. And once a behavior is trained, you shouldn't be giving a treat every time for it, anyway. The same goes for sits, downs, and recalls. Praise your dog for complying, and send her back to play some more, or have a settle-down session if you think one is needed.

You may also be able to use some of the park's features for a little directed jumping exercise. Ask your dog to jump over a log or a bench or whatever offers the correct height for your dog (no higher than shoulder level if you have not practiced jumping). Run with your dog if necessary. Do not, however, ask your dog to jump onto things. Elevated height can lead to problems of feeling more self-assured and becoming pushy, or inviting other dogs to nip at legs now at the height of their mouths.

You can even use your dog's leash as a tug toy, as many agility competitors do. Don't do this if it revs your dog up too much, but if you can do it safely, it's a game most dogs love to play. Keep it short and under control.

Of course some dog parks do permit toys, and in these you'll likely see dogs fetching balls in every direction. Given sufficient space and the right mix of dogs, fetch can be safely played. If the dog park you visit allows toys, by all means bring your tennis ball or flying disc. But before you bring it out to play, be sure you check out all the other dogs in the park. If you know them and have played fetch in their presence before, go ahead and start. If not, then proceed cautiously and keep a watchful eye on any interest shown by another dog in your actions.

Some dog parks have "public" tennis balls scattered about. You may want to bring your own and keep your dog from picking up others, just on the off chance that a dog with some contagious disease has played with the public ball. (See Chapter 7 for a discussion of disease potential in dog parks.)

In dog parks that have swimming water available, people often choose to have their dogs fetch from the water. Labradors and Goldens are the most common enthusiastic participants in this activity. Humans have a couple of added

Many dog parks do allow toys, and some dogs can play happily with them without problems.

responsibilities here. Be sure the water is safe—no strong currents or tidal flows, free of toxic algae (see next chapter), stinging jellyfish, or whatever hazards may be commonly encountered in your geographic area. And watch for other dogs waiting to ambush dogs—look for dogs in an offensive pose nearby staring at the dogs in the water.

Even if you would rather just let your dog do her own thing at the park instead of playing with her yourself, remember that you should call her away from play from time to time. Take a few moments to settle her down, if necessary, then send her back to play some more. The important thing is to stay connected with your dog in whatever way you choose.

Dog parks can sometimes be dog beaches.

Remember To

- Keep moving.
- Keep your eyes and mind focused on what's going on around you.
- Keep your own safety in mind—don't get bowled over by running dogs.
- Be ready to leave at any moment if you see potential problems developing.
- Help your dog stay settled down and in control.
- Politely ask other dog owners to obey the rules.
- Always pick up after your dog.
- Help make the dog park fun for everyone.

Leaving and Going Home

Leaving the dog park is the tricky part for a lot of people. If a visit to the dog park is your dog's main (or, heaven forbid, sole) entertainment, she may be reluctant to leave. If you've done the training advised, you can probably call her to you, but can you keep her with you to exit the gate? Snapping on a leash or dragging the dog by the collar are not good ideas. So how do you get out of the dog park?

One technique is to always pair a fun activity with dog park visits. Maybe after the dog park you go for ice cream cones for both of you. Or you do some doggie massage. Or play with your dog's favorite toy or always have treats available for afterwards. Whatever will condition your dog to see leaving the dog park as forecasting some other reward. But that's in the long-term. What do you do today, while you're trying to get out of the park and your dog is running with her friends and ignoring you?

Practice calling your dog to you in the park, then releasing her to go back and play some more. When it's time to leave, your dog should come along willingly.

You can enlist the help of the other humans. If they can put a stop to play by calling their dogs to them, your dog may be more willing to accompany you out.

You can make a big show of leaving. . .without your dog. Of course you won't really go away and leave your dog unattended in the dog park. But some dogs lose their confident attitude if their human leaves the scene, and your play acting departure may bring your dog looking to go with you.

If you do play tug with your leash, you may be able to entice your dog through the gate while involved in a game of tug.

If you've practiced heeling exercises a lot, you may be able to call your dog to you and off-leash heel her to and through the gate.

Provided there are no other park users needing to use the gate, you may be able to stand with the inner gate open, call your dog to you, and quickly close the inner gate. Then you can safely snap on the leash. Be warned, however, that this will only work once or twice before your dog refuses to come to you if you are near the gate.

But perhaps the solution that may teach you the most is to simply wait for your dog to be finished playing and ready to leave with you. Make the effort to learn how long a time at the dog park seems to satisfy (or tire out!) your dog and then, if possible, try to schedule visits of at least that length.

However you get your dog out of the park, remember to reattach the leash for the walk to the car. You may want to have a settle-down session before you begin the drive home, to help ensure good manners in the car. At home, you can probably depend on your dog taking a nice nap, dreaming of the great time she had at the dog park.

Remember To

- Wait until the gate area is clear.

- Keep safety in mind—don't be in such a hurry to leave that you do something stupid (grab your dog by the collar or drag her by the leash) and risk starting an incident.

- Make leaving the dog park rewarding with some other activity.

- Be sure the gates are latched behind you.

- Reattach your leash once outside the dog park

A tired but happy dog ready to go home after a fun time at the dog park.

Chapter 7
HEALTH ISSUES

Don't be frightened by this chapter. Healthy dogs don't run much more risk of contracting a disease at a dog park than they do when out for a walk in any neighborhood that contains lots of dogs. And while humans can contract a small number of diseases from dogs (most people don't realize this), taking a few common-sense precautions  makes this unlikely to happen. Most of the potential problems we'll discuss can be prevented through vaccinations, pest controls, and de-worming. Prompt cleanup of excrement keeps many diseases from spreading, both among dogs and humans. By taking some simple precautions you'll minimize your chances of contracting or passing on any health problems at the dog park or out in the community.

Air-Borne Diseases

Just like humans, dogs can spray germs into the air when they cough or sneeze. The diseases most likely to be spread this way are **distemper, kennel cough**, and **canine influenza.**

Distemper should not be a worry because all dogs should be vaccinated against it. The vaccine is highly effective against the virus. Note that puppies are not considered adequately protected until seven to ten days after the last puppy vaccination. Boosters will keep your dog's protection up to date and your veterinarian can determine the right schedule for your dog.

Kennel cough is the most common disease encountered at the dog park. Though this is always spoken of as one disease, it can be caused by a variety of both viral and bacterial agents. The available vaccines, sprayed directly into the dog's nose, offer protection only against the *Bordetella bronchiseptica* bacterium, the most common type, and possibly also the canine parainfluenza virus. So even immunized dogs can contract kennel cough, though their odds of avoiding the disease are improved if immunized.

The most notable symptom is a harsh cough, as if the dog is trying to clear something stuck in his throat. Don't take anyone's word that their dog is just coughing on some grass he ate, or because he was pulling on the leash all the way to the dog park. Stay away from any dogs that are coughing. Leave the dog park if you have to. And stay away if your own dog is coughing. The affliction usually runs its course in six weeks. Otherwise healthy dogs usually recover with no ill consequences.

Canine influenza appeared first in racing Greyhounds in 2004 and within a year had spread to pet dogs. Because this is a new disease, dogs have not developed immunity to it, and no vaccine is available. Fortunately, the disease is mild and self-limiting in the majority of cases. Most dogs develop a soft cough (sounding "moist" compared to the harsh dry sound of kennel cough), which lasts for ten to thirty days. They may also have a runny nose, with a thick discharge, and possibly a low-grade fever. The nasal discharge is usually caused by a secondary bacterial infection, and can be treated with a broad-spectrum bactericidal antimicrobial. Some dogs—estimates range from one to five percent—develop a more severe form of canine influenza with a high fever of 104 to 106 degrees (normal is 101 to 102 degrees) and respiratory distress. Most of these cases respond well to antibiotics.

One insidious aspect of the disease is that as many as one-fifth of dogs infected show no clinical symptoms. So they can serve as a source of infection for other dogs for up to ten days, with no one the wiser. Unfortunately this is a risk any dog owner must face unless you want your dog to live in a bubble.

Diseases Spread by Saliva and Urine

Infectious **canine hepatitis** can be transmitted through the saliva or urine of dogs. Water bowls left filled in dog parks could become a disease reservoir, and even "group" tennis balls or other shared toys could pass the disease along.

Canine infectious hepatitis has no relation to human hepatitis, and cannot be transmitted between species. It's highly contagious in dogs, however, and symptoms can appear rapidly. They include high fever, lack of appetite, general malaise, vomiting, diarrhea (often bloody), abdominal pain, and a "tucked up" stomach. Gums may be pale and eyes can become light sensitive, causing squinting.

One of the nastier aspects of the disease is that dogs who have recovered and show no symptoms can continue to shed the virus in their urine for several months. The surest prevention is vaccination.

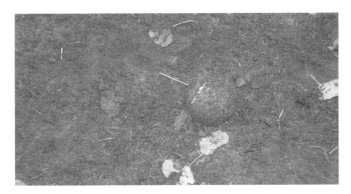

You'll often see tennis balls scattered all over dog parks. It's possible they can spread disease.

Leptospirosis is transmitted via the urine of infected dogs or wild animals such as raccoons or rats. A dog can get the disease simply by sniffing at urine on the ground, or by drinking water contaminated with urine. Some varieties can also be passed along to humans, and lepto is said to be the

Water left out in bowls can be contaminated not just by sick dogs, but by sick wildlife.

most common animal-to-human (called "zoonotic") disease in the world. Vaccination will reduce the severity of the disease, but does not provide immunity from all leptospirosis varieties, and will not prevent infected dogs from becoming carriers.

Symptoms of leptospirosis include sudden fever (103 to 105 degrees), loss of appetite, vomiting, abdominal pain, and refusal to eat. The leptospirosis organism invades the kidneys, resulting in abnormal thirst, frequent urination, darkening in color of urine, and dehydration. Infected dogs need to receive intravenous fluids to maintain hydration while being treated with penicillin and other drugs. "Cured" dogs can excrete the bacteria for as long as several years after infection.

The traditional vaccine for leptospirosis protects against only two of the varieties of the disease and is implicated in the highest risk of side effects among the usual dog vaccines. A newer leptospirosis vaccine immunizes against four varieties, and has been formulated to reduce the potential for side effects. Ask your veterinarian about the advisability of vaccinating your dog. Some vets now routinely use vaccines that don't include lepto, because of the higher potential for side effects. A newer vaccine may change this.

Giardia is a parasite that can be found in the stools of infected animals, and can make its way into open bodies of water. We'll discuss how to avoid this parasite in the section on open water borne diseases

Poop-Borne Problems

The most common potential poop problems include parasites (roundworms, whipworms, hookworms), bacteria (campylobacter, cryptosporidium, salmonella), and one-celled organisms (giardia). All of these can also infect humans.

Roundworms can often be seen in the feces, resembling pieces of spaghetti. They affect the dog's digestive system and lungs, causing vomiting and diarrhea. Heavy infestations can result in convulsions.

Hookworms are tiny bloodsuckers, attaching to the interior intestinal wall and literally sucking blood out of the dog. They are the most devastating of the "worms." Infected dogs become anemic, lethargic, and have dark tar-like feces. Humans can develop a syndrome called cutaneous larva migrans, with the parasites burrowing tunnels under the skin.

Whipworms are also bloodsuckers, with a longer life cycle than the other intestinal parasites. They cause chronic, rather than acute, diarrhea and weight loss. Treatment with dewormers must be carefully timed to eradicate them.

Bacteria in feces aren't unique to the realm of dogs. You've undoubtedly been cautioned to cook ground beef thoroughly to avoid e. coli and not to eat undercooked chicken for fear of salmonella. Bacteria commonly carried in canine feces include campylobacter, cryptosporidium, and salmonella. Symptoms of all include diarrhea, fever, vomiting, and abdominal discomfort.

Canine parvovirus or "parvo" is a potentially life-threatening poop-borne disease that is now rare thanks to highly effective vaccines. Risk of parvo is one of the main reasons you don't want to bring unvaccinated dogs or puppies where there may be risk of the disease—places like parks and dog parks. The virus can remain contagious in the environment for up to a year and disinfection is difficult.

In case you don't already know how to use a bag to pick up poop, some dispensers helpfully offer illustrations.

Preventing the spread of these diseases via poop is straightforward and apply to your back yard as well:

- Always include a fecal examination in your dog's regular veterinary exam. If any parasites are found, your veterinarian can advise you on deworming procedures and any environmental treatment that may be necessary.

- Never touch dog feces with your bare hands (did you really need to be told that?).

- Always clean up feces promptly; keep your hands away from your mouth and eyes after doing so.

- Wash your hands thoroughly as soon as possible. Some say you should lather for at least as long as it takes you to sing a chorus of "Happy Birthday to You."

• Leaving feces in the environment, especially through a rainstorm, allows the germs and/or worms to spread further.

Open Water Borne Diseases

Giardia is another nasty bug, difficult to diagnose and treat, and equally at home in canines and humans. It used to be called "backpacker's disease" because it afflicted those who drank from "pristine" mountain streams, which were infected by beavers or deer or other wildlife with giardia cysts. The problem has become much more widespread in the last twenty years. Encased in a cyst, it can survive for months before an animal drinks it in contaminated water or eats it in feces. Then it develops into the active stage and multiplies in the intestines, where it can cause diarrhea (from mild to explosive), mucousy stools, weight loss, and listlessness. Some dogs remain asymptomatic, but can be carriers, shedding cysts into the environment. To get a diagnosis there needs to be several fecal exams over the course of a week because the cysts are not shed continuously.

Several anti-protozoal drugs are available for treatment, but none kill the encysted form of the parasite, so eradicating it is unlikely. A dog who has been diagnosed with giardia should always be considered to be a carrier and not brought to a dog park. Pick up all poop promptly, and wash your hands thoroughly afterward.

A potentially deadly hazard totally unknown by most people is **a toxic bloom of blue-green algae**. This can happen in still bodies of water, especially if the area around them is fertilized heavily. The blue-green algae, always present in small amounts, suddenly multiply rapidly, or bloom. A bloom containing blue-green algae is not the chunky sort

Water play is a lot of fun, but it can have hazards of its own.

of algae that hangs from a stick you poke into it. A blue-green algae bloom is more like the sheen of oil-based paint floating on top of the water. There is no substance to it.

Blue-green algae are highly toxic, and have forms that attack the liver and forms that attack the nervous system. A bloom in a Washington State lake killed two dogs, while a third barely survived. All dogs swam in the lake and within fifteen minutes went into convulsions. This is an extreme emergency—if your dog shows any central nervous system dysfunction after playing in or drinking water in a lake or pond, rush to a veterinarian. The liver toxin form acts more slowly, but can be just as deadly. Stay away from any water that looks suspicious.

External Parasites

You don't have to go to a dog park to encounter fleas and ticks, of course. But you certainly don't want to be the one responsible for introducing them. Fortunately, flea control has become fast, easy, and effective, and there's no excuse for neglecting this aspect of dog care. Choose your flea control product—chewable tablet or spot-on—and use it regularly. This truly is better living through chemistry.

Tick control requires a little more work. Check all over your dog's body any time you are grooming, and after ventures into woods or fields. Long-coated dogs need special attention because ticks can attach themselves to their coat and eventually find their way to the skin's surface and latch on. Ticks that are removed promptly have little chance to transmit disease. Use tweezers or a tick removal device, grasping the tick as close to the skin as possible and pulling straight back. Drop the tick into alcohol if you want to show it to your veterinarian, or flush it down the toilet.

Ventures into shrubs and woods can result in fleas and ticks hopping aboard. Check your dog after every outing and use preventatives.

Resources

If you want to check out other opinions on dog parks, get advice about forming a group to lobby for a dog park in your area, or learn more about dog parks, check out any of the websites mentioned below that were current at the time of publication.

I have also included resources on dog behavior, training, and canine body language for those who are interested and would like to study the subject further, and on positive training.

Tips for Getting Your Own Dog Park

Dogs are a polarizing creature in our society. As much as you love them and want to provide them a place to run and socialize, there are others just as intent on keeping dogs out of as many public places as possible. To gain any dog-related privileges requires a dedicated group willing to gather information and present it in a fact-based non-confrontational manner to the appropriate governing body. Even if you receive public backing for your park, your group will also either probably need to raise money or solicit donations of materials and labor to help offset land acquisition or construction cost, fund raise to defray maintenance costs, and be responsible for seeing that rules are obeyed and the facility is run well with minimum friction with non-dog owners.

For more details and some plans of action that have already worked for other groups of dog owners, see the following.

www.inch.com/~dogs/runs.html—The website of the American Dog Trainers Network, it includes pages on benefits of dog parks, recommended rules, and "How to Establish a Successful Dog Run in Your Community."

www.akc.org/canine_legislation/dogpark.cfm—A step-by-step guide on starting a dog park that uses the success stories of AKC members as examples of how anyone can start a park.

www.dogpark.com—Includes a section on "Starting a Dog Park," but it actually focuses mostly on design and etiquette/rules and only has a few lines on the role of a dog park group. Other areas of the site are more informative.

www.toppetcare.com/dogparkhowto.html—A short but interesting selection of tips on starting a dog park.

www.dogplay.com—Includes a good discussion on "How Do I Start a Dog Park," with information on promoting the recreational benefits for humans, promoting responsible dog ownership, preparing a show and tell for policymakers, and countering the arguments of anti-dog people.

www.petnet.com.au/openspace/frontis.html—Includes
several pages of reasons dogs need access to public open
space.

s3.phpbbforfree.com/forums/nationaldogpark.html—Offers an ongoing, archived discussion on establishing
a nonprofit organization, fundraising, and looking at
park facilities.

thedogsbestfriend.com/dogpark.htm—Provides a
long, detailed proposal that was made for dog parks
in Santa Barbara. An excellent example to follow, with
pros and cons of dog parks, demographics of the area,
and suggestions on specific areas they considered appropriate for a dog park.

Animal.discovery.com/features/dogpark/startpark/start-
park.html—An Animal Planet article on getting a dog
park, with basic information.

www.ffpp.org—"Establishing a Dog Park in Your Community" discusses how dog parks benefit their communities, how to build a dog park, and offers success
stories.

www.freeplay.org/caseforspace.pdf—A document written
for college credit by students proposing Los Angeles
dog parks, it includes pros and cons, identification of
stakeholders, allocation of park space for dog owners,
criteria, information for those opposed to the idea, and
recommended potential areas.

www.pawparksanford.org—They offer for sale a 340-page
manual "So You Want to Build a Dog Park" for $75.

RESOURCES

Locating Dog Parks

First check out the websites of your local parks departments, which might include town, county, and state, depending on the parks in your vicinity. They will have the most comprehensive information for your area. If you want to venture farther afield, or are traveling with your dog, try these websites:

www.ecoanimal.com/dogfun/—They have a listing of dog parks across the United States and Canada. The listings are supplied by users of the site, so they may be fairly up-to-date and complete for one area and totally nonexistent for another. The listing for Washington state, for example, is extremely spotty.

www.dogpark.com—At the time of this writing, they said they would "soon" have a listing of dog parks in the United States and Canada. They currently do have a calendar of events.

Dog Park Rules and Etiquette

If you want to see what other people have to say about dog park rules and etiquette, here are some websites that discuss these topics.

www.co.greene.oh.us/parks/dog_park_rules.htm—A nice, fairly comprehensive list of dog park rules and etiquette and the basis for each rule.

www.inch.com/~dogs/runs.html—A list of ten of the most common dog park rules.

www.rbdogpark.com/rules.htm—A long list of rules, the reasoning behind them, and suggestions for what to do about inappropriate behavior.

Private Dog Parks

A little bit different than your run-of-the-mill public dog park, these are by membership only. Some of the details on their websites may give you ideas about creating or running a dog park.

> www.royalpaws.com—A location in Atlanta, Georgia, that combines doggy day care with a private 12-acre dog park. Some interesting details

> www.dogwoodpark.com—Another combined doggy day care/private dog park, this one in Gainesville, Florida.

> www.poochiespark.com—A boarding facility combined with a private dog park in Orange Park, Florida.

Dog Socialization

For more background on, and training and management tips regarding keeping dogs sociable, see the following websites.

> www.wagntrain.com/friendly.htm—A page on puppy socialization, bite inhibition, and other exercises to help create a sociable dog.

> www.dogchannel.com/puppies/social/article00002.aspx—Short article on the responsibilities of socializing puppies.

> www.gooddogtraining.com/article_dogparks.htm—Dog park rules, focusing on bringing only socialized dogs to parks.

> www.perfectpaws.com/offleash.html—"When Will I Be Able to Let My Dog Off-Leash?" discusses responsibilities.

Disease and Dog Parks

www.healthypet.com/library_view.aspx?ID-194—Facts about canine influenza, symptoms, and spread.

www.kerryblues.info/index.html?http%3A//www.kerryblues.info/KB/dogpark.html—Article on dogs parks, with a couple of good paragraphs on puppies and disease.

www.peteducation.com/article.cfm?cls=28&cat=1674&articleid=809%20—A long article on dog parks in general, with several paragraphs on disease, parasites, and injuries.

www.clevelandwoman.com/house/vetqa13.htm— A vet answers questions about disease in dog parks, discussing vaccines, fleas, worms, injuries.

Canine Body Language

Only recently have some DVDs become available with visuals and explanations of canine body language. While they are more expensive than the books on the subject, the DVDs have the advantage of actually being able to show the behaviors they are discussing. But both books or the videos can help you learn more about how to interpret the behaviors you are seeing in dogs at the dog park. All are available from Dogwise at www.dogwise.com.

Calming Signals: What Your Dog Tells You, DVD, by Turid Rugaas

Canine Behavior Program: Body Postures & Evaluating Behavioral Health, video, by Suzanne Hetts and Daniel Estep

Canine Body Language, A Photographic Guide, by Brenda Aloff

The Language of Dogs, DVD, by Sarah Kalnajs

On Talking Terms with Dogs: Calming Signals, 2nd edition, (also as DVD Calming Signals), by Turid Rugaas

The Rosetta Bone: The Key to Communication Between Humans and Canines, by Cheryl S. Smith

Stress in Dogs. By Martina Scholz and Clarissa von Reinhardt

Positive Dog Training

I recommend taking some face-to-face training classes with your dog, whether group or private. Working with a knowledgeable dog trainer will make training easier and more successful. Reading can also forward your learning about how to train and why some things work and some things don't. The following all use positive training methods, with the last two being books I have co-written that focus on clicker training and target training—two incredibly successful ways to work with your dog. Again, they are available from Dogwise.

Beginning Family Dog Training, 2nd edition, by Patricia McConnell

Brenda Aloff's Fundamentals: Foundation Training for Every Dog, DVD, by Brenda Aloff

How to Behave So Your Dog Behaves, by Sophia Yin

Outwitting Dogs, by Terry Ryan

The Power of Positive Dog Training, by Pat Miller

Quick Clicks, by Mandy Book and Cheryl S. Smith

Right On Target! by Mandy Book and Cheryl S. Smith

INDEX

Notes:

The Dog Trainer's Resource: The APDT Chronicle of the Dog Collection. Mychelle Blake (*ed*)
Therapy Dogs: Training Your Dog To Reach Others. Kathy Diamond Davis
Training Dogs, A Manual (reprint). Konrad Most
Training the Disaster Search Dog. Shirley Hammond
Try Tracking: The Puppy Tracking Primer. Carolyn Krause
Visiting the Dog Park, Having Fun, and Staying Safe. Cheryl S. Smith
When Pigs Fly. Train Your Impossible Dog. Jane Killion
Winning Team. A Guidebook for Junior Showmanship. Gail Haynes
Working Dogs (reprint). Elliot Humphrey & Lucien Warner

HEALTH & ANATOMY, SHOWING
An Eye for a Dog. Illustrated Guide to Judging Purebred Dogs. Robert Cole
Annie On Dogs! Ann Rogers Clark
Canine Cineradiography DVD. Rachel Page Elliott
Canine Massage: A Complete Reference Manual. Jean-Pierre Hourdebaigt
Canine Terminology (reprint). Harold Spira
Dog In Action (reprint). Macdowell Lyon
Dogsteps DVD. Rachel Page Elliott
Performance Dog Nutrition: Optimize Performance With Nutrition. Jocelynn Jacobs
Puppy Intensive Care: A Breeder's Guide To Care Of Newborn Puppies. Myra Savant Harris
Raw Dog Food: Make It Easy for You and Your Dog. Carina MacDonald
Raw Meaty Bones. Tom Lonsdale
Shock to the System. The Facts About Animal Vaccination... Catherine O'Driscoll
The History and Management of the Mastiff. Elizabeth Baxter & Pat Hoffman
Work Wonders. Feed Your Dog Raw Meaty Bones. Tom Lonsdale
Whelping Healthy Puppies, DVD. Sylvia Smart